HEARING THE MESSAGE
OF HABAKKUK

LIVING BY FAITH IN A VIOLENT WORLD

CHRISTOPHER J. H. WRIGHT

ZONDERVAN

Hearing the Message of Habakkuk
Copyright © 2024 by Christopher J. H. Wright

Published in Grand Rapids, Michigan, by Zondervan. Zondervan is a registered trademark of The Zondervan Corporation, L.L.C., a wholly owned subsidiary of HarperCollins Christian Publishing, Inc.

Requests for information should be addressed to customercare@harpercollins.com.

Zondervan titles may be purchased in bulk for educational, business, fundraising, or sales promotional use. For information, please email SpecialMarkets@Zondervan.com.

ISBN 978-0-310-14750-3 (audio)

Library of Congress Cataloging-in-Publication Data

Names: Wright, Christopher J. H., 1947- author.
Title: Hearing the message of Habakkuk : living by faith in a violent world / Christopher J. H. Wright.
Description: Grand Rapids, Michigan : Zondervan, [2024] | Includes index.
Identifiers: LCCN 2023056013 (print) | LCCN 2023056014 (ebook) | ISBN 9780310147480 (paperback) | ISBN 9780310147497 (ebook)
Subjects: LCSH: Bible. Habakkuk—Criticism, interpretation, etc. | BISAC: RELIGION / Biblical Studies / Old Testament / Prophets | RELIGION / Faith
Classification: LCC BS1635.52 .W75 2024 (print) | LCC BS1635.52 (ebook) | DDC 224/.9506—dc23/eng/20240110
LC record available at https://lccn.loc.gov/2023056013
LC ebook record available at https://lccn.loc.gov/2023056014

Unless otherwise noted, Scripture quotations are taken from The Holy Bible, New International Version®, NIV®. Copyright © 1973, 1978, 1984, 2011 by Biblica, Inc.® Used by permission of Zondervan. All rights reserved worldwide. www.Zondervan.com. The "NIV" and "New International Version" are trademarks registered in the United States Patent and Trademark Office by Biblica, Inc.®

Scripture quotations marked ESV are taken from the ESV® Bible (The Holy Bible, English Standard Version®). Copyright © 2001 by Crossway, a publishing ministry of Good News Publishers. Used by permission. All rights reserved.

Scripture quotations marked KJV are taken from the King James Version. Public domain.

Scripture quotations marked MSG are taken from *THE MESSAGE*. Copyright © 1993, 2002, 2018 by Eugene H. Peterson. Used by permission of NavPress. All rights reserved. Represented by Tyndale House Publishers, Inc.

Scripture quotations marked NLT are taken from the Holy Bible, New Living Translation. © 1996, 2004, 2015 by Tyndale House Foundation. Used by permission of Tyndale House Publishers, Inc., Carol Stream, Illinois 60188. All rights reserved.

Any internet addresses (websites, blogs, etc.) and telephone numbers in this book are offered as a resource. They are not intended in any way to be or imply an endorsement by Zondervan, nor does Zondervan vouch for the content of these sites and numbers for the life of this book.

Cover design: Studio Gearbox
Cover photo: © Oversnap / Getty Images
Interior design: Kait Lamphere
Interior Typesetting: Sara Colley

Printed in the United States of America

24 25 26 27 28 29 30 31 32 33 34 / TRM / 16 15 14 13 12 11 10 9 8 7 6 5 4 3 2 1

"Discussions about the problem of evil run the risk of being solely intellectual endeavors, detached from human suffering and disconnected from the resources of the gospel. By contrast, in this powerful and moving book Chris Wright wisely and insightfully engages the problem of evil in its ancient setting. He illuminates the message of the prophet Habakkuk, who himself was wrestling with the existential threat of the coming Babylonian invasion. Wright offers this apt summary: 'We may not understand the *world* we are in, but we do know the *story* we are in. And we need to strengthen our faith by continually bringing this story to mind'—which is precisely what the prophet Habakkuk himself was doing."

   —PAUL COPAN, Pledger Family Chair of Philosophy and Ethics and professor of philosophy and ethics, Palm Beach Atlantic University, Florida, author of *Loving Wisdom: A Guide to Philosophy and Christian Faith* and *Is God a Vindictive Bully?*

"Chris has done it once more! One of our generation's most careful and thoughtful biblical scholars and church leaders applies theological insight, biblical understanding, and pastoral concern to the book of Habakkuk, opening it up for our day. His attentiveness offers a fresh word from an indispensable prophetic book. As I preach and teach Habakkuk, I will return to this gift again and again."

   —HEATH A. THOMAS, president and professor of Old Testament, Oklahoma Baptist University, associate fellow, the Kirby Laing Centre for Public Theology in Cambridge

"Chris Wright has become a trustworthy and reliable interpreter of Scripture for many in our day. He is a fine scholar fully in command of the tools of biblical scholarship. Additionally, he is also pastorally sensitive, able to hear God's address to our present context as it shapes a faithful missional people for the sake of the world. I am always delighted when Chris takes on another canonical book; this brief commentary will apply the Word of God to our day, whether it guides the preacher or a group Bible study or one's personal reading."

—**MICHAEL GOHEEN**, professor of missional theology, Calvin Theological Seminary and Missional Training Center

"Here is a book for such a time as this. With customary clarity, Chris Wright unpacks the extraordinary relevance of Habakkuk to the unsettling realities of our world, pointing us to the certainties of God's sovereign control and compassionate care. Each chapter draws illuminating applications from across Scripture and Christian experience, pastorally encouraging us in the midst of troubling times, strengthening our faith, and inserting vertebra in our elastic spines."

—**JONATHAN LAMB**, author and teacher, former director of Langham Preaching

"Chris Wright, a biblical theologian and steward of words, navigates us through the dark days of Habakkuk, comparing them to the turbulent geopolitical history of our own times. We learn context and history, and even 'feel' with Habakkuk. Thankfully, although we are challenged and slightly provoked as we journey through Habakkuk's book, Chris adeptly brings us through to its gloriously hopeful last chapter. There, he unfolds the sagely kind of wisdom I've come to expect from him—'we live every day in renewed trust in the sovereign good governance of God in God's world.' I could discern that word of faith on every page."

—**KIM THOMAS**, artist, author, and curate at The Village Chapel, Nashville, Tennessee

HEARING THE MESSAGE
of HABAKKUK

To Riad Kassis
International Director, Langham Partnership
And a fellow wrestler with the book of Habakkuk

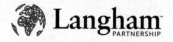

CONTENTS

PREFACE

One of the earliest "serious books" I remember reading as a Christian teenager was Martyn Lloyd-Jones's exposition of Habakkuk, *From Fear to Faith: Rejoicing in the Lord in Turbulent Times*. It had been first published by IVP in 1953 (when I was six!), and it seemed to grow in powerful relevance in the ruins of Europe after the Second World War and then the fear-filled years of the Cold War, including the nuclear arms race and the Cuban Missile Crisis in 1962. Those were indeed the "turbulent times" of my teens. Encountering Habakkuk through the sharp Lloyd-Jones lens had a stabilizing and strengthening impact on my youthful faith (and also sowed the seeds of my love for the Old Testament Scriptures and their powerful relevance; but that's another story).

However, Habakkuk is a book that seems perennially relevant, since the world the prophet describes is familiar in so many eras of human history, including our own (increasingly so, one might say). It was (and still is) a world of national wickedness and international turmoil and violence—a world in which God *appears* to be asleep on his watch and yet *claims* to be "working a work" in Habakkuk's day and ours.

So, now, a long way from my teens and as I grow older in this ever more turbulent world, I genuinely feel fearful about what kind of world my grandchildren (some already in their own teenage years) will inherit for perhaps the next half century of their lives (unless the Lord returns before then). With such thoughts, I find that Habakkuk's own turbulent mixture of questions, protest, affirmation, fear, faith, and gritty determination to press on also speaks for my heart.

I am grateful to the Maidstone Bible Week for inviting me to share expositions of Habakkuk during its yearly meetings in May 2018. What follows in this book is substantially an expansion of what I delivered on those evenings. Thus, it is important to say that this small book does not pretend to be a *commentary* on Habakkuk, in the full technical sense of that word. It is, rather, an attempt simply to let Habakkuk's message speak again today as it did two and a half millennia ago. Such is the amazing power of the living word of God.

Among the commentaries that I have found helpful, along with Martyn Lloyd-Jones's exposition, are these:

Baker, David W. *Nahum, Habakkuk and Zephaniah*. Tyndale Old Testament Commentaries. Downers Grove: IVP, 2009.

Prior, David. *The Message of Joel, Micah and Habakkuk*. The Bible Speaks Today. Leicester, UK: IVP, 1998 (rev. ed. forthcoming later in 2024 from IVP Academic).

Lamb, Jonathan. *From Why to Worship: An Introduction to the Book of Habakkuk*. Carlisle, UK: Langham, 2018 (previously published by Authentic Media, 2007).

Kassis, Riad A. *Frustrated with God: A Syrian Theologian's Reflections on Habakkuk*. San Bernardino, CA: CreateSpace, 2016.

Thomas, Heath A. *Faith Amid the Ruins: The Book of Habakkuk*. Transformative Word. Bellingham, WA: Lexham, 2016.

INTRODUCTION

We know nothing about Habakkuk beyond what we read in his book. But don't let that discourage you, since he opens his heart wide enough for us to feel like we know him.

He calls himself "Habakkuk the prophet," which may have been his official title, perhaps as one of the temple prophets (unlike Amos, who distinguished himself from that guild; Amos 7:14–15). He writes a song with musical directions in chapter 3, which might imply that he had some kind of professional role, though other prophets were certainly very capable of composing poetry and singing songs.

Like all prophets, Habakkuk receives a word from God. And, like some other prophets, he is prepared to answer back to God! Indeed, the first word Habakkuk receives *from* God is in answer to a complaint he had first addressed *to* God. It seems Habakkuk was banging on God's door before God got a word in. So he is a man of amazing boldness in his encounters with God and, as we shall see, a man of incredible faith.

When did Habakkuk live? Unlike some prophets, Habakkuk does not date his words to any particular king of Israel or Judah. However, he describes an era of rampant moral and social evil among his own people, and he is given a vision of the rapid rise of the Babylonian Empire (1:6), which happened under Nebuchadnezzar. These two facts fit well with the closing decades of the kingdom of Judah, particularly the reign of King Jehoiakim (reigned 609–598 BC).

Habakkuk is, therefore, probably a contemporary of Jeremiah—whose prophetic ministry began during the reign of

the good king Josiah and lasted forty years through the reigns of
Jehoiakim, Jehoiachin, and Zedekiah, right up to and beyond the
587 BC siege and destruction of Jerusalem and into the Babylonian
exilic period. Habakkuk's ministry may have been much shorter,
but we have no way of knowing how long he was active since all
we have are these short chapters of his book. However, it is at
least clear that the issue Habakkuk brings before God (the rise of
Babylon) and God's answer to him must have happened sometime
in the early reign of Jehoiakim, when the great Babylonian threat
was looming on the horizon.

So, let's look at what the world was like in Habakkuk's day,
first in the world of international empires and then nationally in
the small kingdom of Judah.

Internationally: The Assyrian Empire, which had ruled the
whole region for almost a hundred and fifty years, was beginning to
collapse. This was the empire which, during the reign of Hezekiah,
had attacked and besieged Jerusalem in 701 BC. At that time God

had brought about a miraculous deliverance, as the prophet Isaiah had described (Isa 36–37). In spite of that one setback, however, the Assyrian Empire had carried on, seemingly invincible. But all empires eventually begin to collapse under their own weight and God's judgment.

In 627 BC the great Assyrian king Ashurbanipal died. He was the last really strong king of that empire—and in that same year God called young Jeremiah to be his prophet. Both of these things happened during the thirteenth year of the reign of Josiah (Jer 1:2). Josiah was the king who, out of a renewed loyalty to Yahweh, the God of Israel, was pursuing a policy of increasing resistance to Assyria, seeking to reestablish Judah's independence and pursue religious reformation (2 Kgs 22–23).

Tragically, however, in 609 BC King Josiah was killed in the Battle of Megiddo. He had been foolishly trying to prevent the Egyptian army from going to the aid of the Assyrians against the new rising power—Babylon. The Egyptian army defeated Judah, Josiah was killed (and greatly mourned), and Judah came under the power of Egypt—but not for long.

In 605 BC, at the Battle of Carchemish a good distance north of Judah, Nebuchadnezzar, king of Babylon, decisively defeated the Egyptian–Assyrian coalition and established Babylonian power over the whole region. This meant the end of the Assyrian Empire and the beginning of the Babylonian Empire, which would last approximately another seventy years. In that same year (605 BC), Nebuchadnezzar briefly besieged Jerusalem—probably as a warning against further rebellion (which Judah didn't heed). Some people were taken off into exile at that time, including Daniel and his three friends (Dan 1:1–2). So, from 605 BC the kingdom of Judah became a vassal state of the Babylonian Empire, along with other small nations in that region.

For several decades, then, the whole world of the ancient Near East had been in turmoil, with one empire collapsing and another rising to take its place. All of this was generating great fear and uncertainty, especially among the smaller nations who, like Judah, had got caught up in the rivalry of the great powers of Egypt and Mesopotamia. As the African saying goes: when elephants fight, the grass gets trampled. Habakkuk turns to God in the midst of that world—a world he could not understand—with those fears and questions tormenting his mind.

Nationally: Although King Josiah had made valiant efforts to bring about reformation in Judah, the country was still suffering the long-term legacy of the evil reign of King Manasseh (reigned 687–640 BC). During that long reign, the people had slid into increasing idolatry and evil practices of all kinds. Here is part of the biblical account of Manasseh's reign.

> [1]Manasseh was twelve years old when he became king, and he reigned in Jerusalem fifty-five years. His mother's name was Hephzibah. [2]He did evil in the eyes of the LORD, following the detestable practices of the nations the LORD had driven out before the Israelites. [3]He rebuilt the high places his father Hezekiah had destroyed; he also erected altars to Baal and made an Asherah pole, as Ahab king of Israel had done. He bowed down to all the starry hosts and worshiped them. [4]He built altars in the temple of the LORD, of which the LORD had said, "In Jerusalem I will put my Name." [5]In the two courts of the temple of the LORD, he built altars to all the starry hosts. [6]He sacrificed his own son in the fire, practiced divination, sought omens, and consulted mediums and spiritists. He did much evil in the eyes of the LORD, arousing his anger. . . .
>
> Moreover, Manasseh also shed so much innocent blood that he filled Jerusalem from end to end—besides the sin that he had caused Judah to commit, so that they did evil in the eyes of the LORD. (2 Kgs 21:1–6, 16)

Even though Josiah had achieved some major reforms and purged the nation of the outward trappings of other gods, he was soon followed by his son Jehoiakim, who tragically reversed Josiah's policies and behaved in arrogant, ostentatious, and oppressive ways. This is Jeremiah's verdict on Jehoiakim in comparison with his father, the good king Josiah:

> ¹³"Woe to him who builds his palace by
>   unrighteousness,
>   his upper rooms by injustice,
> making his own people work for nothing,
>   not paying them for their labor.
> ¹⁴He says, 'I will build myself a great palace
>   with spacious upper rooms.'
> So he makes large windows in it,
>   panels it with cedar
>   and decorates it in red.
>
> ¹⁵"Does it make you a king
>   to have more and more cedar?
> Did not your father [i.e., Josiah] have food and drink?
>   He did what was right and just,
>   so all went well with him.
> ¹⁶He defended the cause of the poor and needy,
>   and so all went well.
> Is that not what it means to know me?"
>   declares the LORD.
> ¹⁷"But your eyes and your heart
>   are set only on dishonest gain,
> on shedding innocent blood
>   and on oppression and extortion."
>   (Jer 22:13–17)

As I said earlier, it was probably during the reign of Jehoiakim when Habakkuk asked his questions and got his disturbing answers. What a time it was, then!

- **Socially and economically:** There was increasing poverty, social inequality, sexual dysfunction, arrogant exploitation by the "elite," dispossession, and all the suffering that went with loss of land and security (cf. Jer 7 and 22). The country of Judah was descending into a spiral of increasing degradation and wickedness, while the perpetrators of these ills were boldly getting away with it. That was the trigger for Habakkuk's opening complaint to God, as we shall see.

- **Religiously:** There was a mixture of syncretistic worship of other gods (Jer 2) and concurrently a paradoxically dangerous complacency in the assurance that Yahweh, the God of Israel, would always defend his city. God's people would be safe as long as they carried on their worship in the Lord's temple, for God would never allow his own temple to be destroyed. How wrong they were (Jer 7)!

- **Politically:** Because the international scene was so turbulent, the political alignment of Judah oscillated back and forth. There was apparently constant conflict between the anti-Babylonian and pro-Babylonian parties in Jerusalem. Jeremiah suffered badly at the hands of the former party, since he went around saying that God had raised up Nebuchadnezzar (just as God had told Habakkuk) and the best thing to do for the moment was to submit to that king. This was subversive speech which made Jeremiah very unpopular, to say the least. Jeremiah consequently narrowly escaped lynching and murder more than once. Other prophets were not so fortunate—check out Uriah (Jer 26:20–23). Speaking truth to power was dangerous!

So, then, Habakkuk lived at a time and in a world with many similarities to our own. There were frightening international tensions, the decline of one superpower and the rise of another, attendant anxiety and fear among smaller nations that tended to get trampled in the conflicts, and the confusion of political alignments and alliances. And, at the same time, the fracturing of moral and religious bonds and traditions were plaguing Judah's own society with social dissolution and degradation. "Confusing" is a mild world for all this—it was international, political, religious, and moral chaos and rampant unchecked evil.

It was a bad time. It was a baffling time. It was a world that was hard to understand. What did Habakkuk have to say about this situation? More importantly, what did God have to say about it?

Today, it is more than three-quarters of a century since the end of the Second World War, and in that time (my own lifetime) we have seen:

- the frightening paranoia of the Cold War—and then its ending;
- the imposition and then the removal of apartheid in South Africa;
- the collapse of the Soviet Union, and then Russia's recovery of global influence;
- the rise of China to increasing economic and political prominence;
- the Arab Spring alongside the counterforce of the rise of ISIS and Islamic extremism;
- the rise of authoritarian, populist, dictatorial, and violent regimes in several countries around the world;
- The phenomena of Donald Trump in the USA and Boris Johnson and Brexit in the UK;
- the humiliating debacle of Western forces in Afghanistan after twenty years;
- the waves and waves of refugees and migrants, fleeing from war, famine, climate disasters, and genocide;
- humanitarian catastrophes in Yemen, for the Rohingya people of Myanmar, in Ethiopia, etc. . . .
- the spiralling threat of climate chaos and global warming;

- the devastation of the global COVID-19 pandemic and the way it has exposed and exacerbated the massive inequalities and injustices that still persist both between and within our countries;
- the Russian invasion of Ukraine and the devastating human, infrastructural, and ecological damage it has caused;
- the renewed outbreak of war in Israel, unprecedented for decades in its violence.

And the list goes on. It is a frightening world, and who can understand it?

How does Habakkuk help us in any way, as we struggle to work out in our day what it means to believe in God's sovereignty, justice, and love? How can we live as faithful disciples of the Lord Jesus Christ in the midst of a violent and unjust world? Let's journey with Habakkuk through the questions he asked and the jaw-dropping answers he received.

CHAPTER 1

QUESTIONING GOD'S SILENCE: WHEN GOD TAKES NO ACTION *AGAINST* EVIL PEOPLE

Habakkuk 1:1–4

Habakkuk is unusual among the prophets. Surprisingly, he does not start out with a word from God to deliver to the people; rather, he begins with a word of his own delivered to God. Habakkuk launches straight into a debate with God. In this he is rather like Job, who refuses to stifle his feelings or his questions:

> Therefore I will not keep silent;
>> I will speak out in the anguish of my spirit,
>> I will complain in the bitterness of my soul. (Job 7:11)

Job was worried, however, that he would come off worse in any argument (not that it stopped him trying!):

> ¹⁴How then can I dispute with him?
>> How can I find words to argue with him?
> ¹⁵Though I were innocent, I could not answer him;
>> I could only plead with my Judge for mercy.
> ¹⁶Even if I summoned him and he responded,
>> I do not believe he would give me a hearing.
> ¹⁷He would crush me with a storm
>> and multiply my wounds for no reason.

1

[18]He would not let me catch my breath
>   but would overwhelm me with misery.
[19]If it is a matter of strength, he is mighty!
>   And if it is a matter of justice, who can challenge him?
>   (Job 9:14–19)

Habakkuk doesn't seem to have any such fears or inhibitions. He will bend God's ear until he gets an answer.

Jeremiah is likewise very bold to put straight questions and complaints to God:

> You are always righteous, LORD,
>   when I bring a case before you.
> Yet I would speak with you about your justice:
>   Why does the way of the wicked prosper?
>   Why do all the faithless live at ease? (Jer 12:1)

> Why is my pain unending
>   and my wound grievous and incurable?
> You are to me like a deceptive brook,
>   like a spring that fails. (Jer 15:18)

It is indeed a remarkable feature of the Bible that God allows (and records) questions like these. Some questions arise from sinful rebellion against God, as when Cain gruffly asks God if he is supposed to be his brother's keeper (Gen 4:9).

But many other questions come from faithful servants of God who cannot understand God's ways at some particular moment. Those questions are often agonizing or despairing. Moses, Elijah, and many psalmists hurl questions at God on various occasions.

And, of course, the most profound question of all is when Jesus, in the depth of his agony on the cross, bearing the weight of human sin (including all the things Habakkuk protested about), has the opening question of Psalm 22 speak for him right then: "My God, my God, why have you forsaken me?"

So, if you find yourself sometimes wracked with questions, unable to see a way to sort them all out in your head, and perhaps questioning God himself . . . then, quite frankly and quite biblically, you are in very good company! Take heart and read on.

HABAKKUK'S COMPLAINT (1:2–4)

> *2How long, LORD, must I call for help,*
> *but you do not listen?*
> *Or cry out to you, "Violence!"*
> *but you do not save?*
> *3Why do you make me look at injustice?*
> *Why do you tolerate wrongdoing?*
> *Destruction and violence are before me;*
> *there is strife, and conflict abounds.*
> *4Therefore the law is paralyzed,*
> *and justice never prevails.*
> *The wicked hem in the righteous,*
> *so that justice is perverted. (1:2–4)*

Habakkuk asks two questions. The first begins, "*How long . . . ?*" (v. 2), and the second begins, "*Why . . . ?*" (v. 3). And then he follows his two questions with a statement that is virtually an accusation against God himself, "*Therefore . . .*" (v. 4). This is all very raw and pointed—God needs to listen up.

It feels like this is an explosion of emotions at the end of a long period of wrestling with the issues Habakkuk mentions. "*How long . . . ?*" suggests that he has been crying out to God for a long time already and has been waiting for an answer—but is getting none. This is an experience familiar to many believers.

"*How long . . . ?*" sounds like, "I have my limits, Lord. I can't go on with all this pain and suffering and anguish, if you don't answer me soon."

"*Why . . . ?*" sounds like, "I need some answers, some reasons, some *explanation*. It all seems so senseless and contradictory. Please tell me why all this is happening. I just don't understand the world around me."

God's silence seems so thick that Habakkuk cannot get through to him, and he cannot bear this any longer. His book bursts onto our ears with these agonized questions and painful observations.

Let's look a little more closely at Habakkuk's complaints. He can't understand why God is not doing what he can and should do. And he can't understand why God seems oblivious to things that God himself condemns. Has God become blind or impotent?

God Is Not Doing What Habakkuk Knows God Can Do (1:2)

First of all, God can and should *listen*, but he is not doing that now (v. 2a):

> How long, LORD, must I call for help,
>   but you do not listen?

Habakkuk knows that Yahweh, the LORD God of Israel, is the God who listens. That was the trigger for the greatest event in Israel's history. The great story of the exodus begins when God *hears* the crying out of his people, sees their misery in slavery, and has compassion on them. Yahweh is the listening God:

> [23b]The Israelites groaned in their slavery and cried out, and their cry for help because of their slavery went up to God. [24]God heard their groaning and he remembered his covenant with Abraham, with Isaac and with Jacob. [25]So God looked on the Israelites and was concerned about them. (Exod 2:23b–25)

Habakkuk would have known psalms like this one, and wished it could be true for him:

> In my distress I called to the LORD;
> > I cried to my God for help.
> From his temple he heard my voice;
> > my cry came before him, into his ears.
> > > (Ps 18:6)

Habakkuk's cry sounds much more like this familiar cry:

> ¹My God, my God, why have you forsaken me?
> > Why are you so far from saving me,
> > so far from my cries of anguish?
> ²My God, I cry out by day, but you do not answer,
> > by night, but I find no rest. (Ps 22:1–2)

There are times when this is the experience of any believer. We sing again and again, calling out to God,[1] but no matter how much we believe God hears our prayers, it still *feels* as if he is not listening at all.

I remember a period of my own life when it seemed God would not answer my prayers. Or, rather, it was a time when God *did* answer my prayers for other people, sometimes in very beautiful and moving ways, but would not answer my prayers for myself in a very specific need and longing. This can be a hard and lonely and testing time.

And then, secondly, Habakkuk complains that God can and should **save**, but he is not doing this either:

> *Or cry out to you, "Violence!"*
> > *but you do not save? (v. 2b)*

---

1. Such as in the song "Faithful One, So Unchanging," by Brian Doerksen.

Habakkuk knows for certain that Yahweh is the God who saves. That fact defined the whole story of his own people. Indeed, Yahweh's power to save is one of his defining characteristics. "The LORD is the God of my salvation" is the exclamation in so many psalms. And this preeminent quality and ability of God was also demonstrated unmistakably and unforgettably at the exodus. That was why the name of Yahweh was forever associated with this event, along with all the vocabulary of salvation, deliverance, redemption, rescue, liberation, and so on. The Hebrew language has as many words as English for the act of bringing people up out of suffering, danger, and death. And one of those salvation words, of course, is immortalized in the name given to God's own Son, *Jesus*—the Greek form of the Hebrew name Yeshua or Yehoshua (Joshua), meaning "the Lord saves." No wonder that Simeon exclaimed, "My eyes have seen *your salvation*," as he cuddled the saving God nestling there as a tiny baby in his arms (Luke 2:30; my italics).

So, that's agreed, then.

God saved his whole people out of the violence of Egypt. And God saved many psalmists from the violence of their enemies. Take a look, for example at Psalms 3, 13, 18, 30, 40, and so forth. You get the gist. Habakkuk knew all those stories and Scriptures. Yahweh is the saving God.

BUT, says Habakkuk, all I see is "*Violence!*" all around me. I've been crying out to God about it for a long time, but he does *not* save the victims. Where is this saving God when you need him? Where is this saving God when others need him and you plead with him on their behalf? Is all God's saving work only in the past? Does he not care about the victims of violence and oppression in our current world? I have all too often been tempted to wonder this myself, overwhelmed by the news of yet another outbreak of horrendous genocidal violence or the exposure of the vicious enslavement in the backbreaking, heartbreaking destitution of so many millions in our world.

The word "violence" (*hamas*) is a key word in this book. It occurs six times, including in the list in Habakkuk 1:3. In 1:2 it is a kind of yell—a cry for help. It's like the shout of somebody witnessing a brutal attack on some innocent victim nearby and shouting out, hoping that others, or the police, will come to intervene.

This, then, is the opening salvo of Habakkuk's complaint. The God he knows and worships and trusts is Yahweh. And Yahweh is the just and compassionate God who characteristically listens and saves. Yahweh is the God who hears the cry of the victims of violence and saves them. All the old stories of Israel's history illustrate this truth. Many psalms celebrate it.

But right now? God is *not* listening nor saving. These are the two things that God has done in the past, that God can do at any time, that God *should* do . . . but is *not* doing now. God is neither listening to Habakkuk nor saving the victims of violence.

Here, then, is the challenge of verse 2. It seems there is a contradiction between what Habakkuk knows and believes about God from the stories, the Scriptures, and the worship songs of his people on the one hand and the present reality that surrounds him on the other. There is a clash between what he believes and what he sees. And God has been silent and inactive for so long. How much longer do Habakkuk (and others) have to cry out before God hears and saves them? But God just goes on doing nothing, it seems.

This leads to the second question. Habakkuk shifts from *How long?* to *Why?*

God Is Doing Nothing about the Things God Himself Condemns (1:3)

> *Why do you make me look at injustice?*
> *Why do you tolerate wrongdoing?*
> *Destruction and violence are before me;*
> *there is strife, and conflict abounds. (1:3)*

What are the things that God *ought* to be doing something about, but isn't? Habakkuk has a list! He reels off six different words for social evils of all sorts. Habakkuk piles them up one after the other in quick succession, like a hysterical TV commentator on some terrible scene of carnage. The sheer catalogue of such words should make us realize that this is a very serious complaint. Habakkuk has thought everything through. He has observed what's going on around him, and it is horrible—there are hardly enough words to describe it. But he's got six words at least, and they are pretty strong.

Here are these words in the order they come in verse 3, with their NIV translation and then a broader sense of each word's meaning.

'awen	"injustice"	trouble, wickedness, looming disaster
'amal	"wrongdoing"	mischief, sorrow, suffering caused to others
sôd	"destruction"	violent devastation, murderous assault, ruin
hamas	"violence"	ruthless physical abuse, serious injury, mistreatment, weapons
rîb	"strife"	court cases, litigation, contention, disputes
madôn	"conflict"	quarrelling, contention, scolding, argument

These are the marks of a sick and decadent society. These are words you could use when the crime rate is escalating. Anti-social behaviour is becoming routine. Violence is happening on the streets. Society is divided against itself in constant litigation and contention. Economic chaos and endless political arguing and fighting are raging, with no solution. And, in the midst of everything, ordinary people are suffering and afraid. This may sound like a very modern picture (and it is), but that was the Judah Habakkuk observed. And other prophets like Jeremiah agreed.

It's noticeable that Habakkuk does not merely use a generic word like "sin" (for which Hebrew also had several words). All of us are individual sinners in one way and another, "in thought and word and deed, through negligence, through weakness, through our own deliberate fault," as the Anglican prayer of confession puts it. But Habakkuk is not just thinking of how bad all of us are as sinners in general.

What Habakkuk describes are *the social outworkings of sin* in the community. These are the kind of things that take root and flourish in society, which they have done from the earliest days of our human history. These are aspects of society gone rotten. These are evils that embed themselves in the structures and practices of fallen human societies, in ways that of course involve individual sinful acts but compound and amplify them in ways that cause massive suffering on all sides.

Very early on, the Bible gives us some devastating verdicts on the human race and our inexhaustible capacity for giving expression to our sin:

> The LORD saw how great the wickedness of the human race had become on the earth, and that every inclination of the thoughts of the human heart was only evil all the time. (Gen 6:5)

> Now the earth was corrupt in God's sight and was full of violence. (Gen 6:11)

> . . . every inclination of the human heart is evil from childhood. (Gen 8:21)

The rest of the Old Testament makes it very clear that these are things that God abhors. The Law, the Prophets, the Narratives, the

Psalms, and the Wisdom Literature all condemn the way human beings fight and squabble, hate and kill, and oppress and exploit one another.

God hates all this.

Habakkuk knows this. So it's hard enough for Habakkuk himself to have to "look at" all these things, merely as a human observer and also as a fellow sinner. Why does God make him see all this? That's what he asks: "*Why do you* **make** *me look at injustice?*" (v. 3a; my emphasis). He feels like some naughty child whose parents turn him around and force him to look at the mess of his bedroom.

But, far worse, how can *God himself* "*idly look at wrong*" (v. 3a ESV)? Habakkuk knows all about God's holiness, after all. That attribute in itself will become another problem in verse 13. So, how does this holy God "tolerate" the accumulating evils of human society, as it seems to go from bad to worse? How can God go on looking at what happens on earth as if it didn't matter to him? Why does God apparently do nothing about things he utterly and totally hates? Why?

So, these are Habakkuk's two primary questions hurled at God—"How long?" (v. 2) and "Why?" (v. 3).

But, then, Habakkuk slams in the conclusion. Since all those things are happening in society, it is painfully obvious that the whole moral order is turned upside down. So that's where he goes next, as we read in verse 4.

God's Moral Order Is Impotent and Perverted (1:4)

"Therefore," concludes Habakkuk (that is, precisely because you, God, are doing nothing), two results happen:

1. **"The law is paralyzed."** By "the law," Habakkuk is referring to the Torah, or what we call the Pentateuch—the first five books of the Bible. This was God's guidance for Israel. This is where God had provided a comprehensive

pattern for their national life, with narratives that showed so clearly right from wrong, explicit instructions, some detailed legislation, and multiple motivations and warnings—all wrapped in the story of God's redeeming love and salvation. That was the massive gift of God's grace to his people—his Torah for their guidance and blessing. Check out Psalm 19 for how precious it was. But all this has now become cold and numb, paralyzed and impotent. God's word has been "frozen out" by the people it was given to. Now it is being deliberately flouted with apparent impunity. Nobody cares what God says (or said) anymore. It's all just a dead letter, irrelevant in everyday life. If that was a painful sight for Habakkuk, how much more was it for the God who had given his people this treasure house of scriptural guidance? God's living and active word . . . paralyzed.

2. **"Justice never prevails."** Justice is the proper application of good laws by those in authority. Justice is the responsibility of judges, rulers, kings, and governments. Justice is, in fact, the very thing God most expects from such human authorities, and is also the thing that the rest of society is entitled to expect and should be able to receive from these authorities. But, now, justice never wins. Justice has been replaced by anarchy. Or, rather, even when some apparent "justice" is done, it is actually "perverted." Literally, Habakkuk says, "justice goes forth, but bent, twisted, crooked." This is the language of corruption, the phenomenon that "you get the justice you pay for." So, even when there are those who may *wish* to do justice ("the righteous"), they are outnumbered, surrounded, and "hemmed in" by those who wield all the influence of wealth and have powerful vested interests in making sure that injustice prevails—for their own benefit. Again, the shockingly modern echoes are not hard to hear.

As a result of these twin evils, the whole way in which God wants human society to work (with those in authority doing justice on behalf of those who are in need) has been turned upside down. God's law is still there, but it is useless and impotent. Those who *should* see that justice is done are complicit in making sure that justice is *not* done.

Thus, Habakkuk lodges his complaint.

He is pouring out his protest to God. Habakkuk does this because he assumes that God really does still care about the same things as he does, but he is unable to understand why God goes on allowing such things to continue.

Habakkuk is living in very bad times. He is a person of moral sensitivity. He is desperately troubled by all that is going on in his own land and among his own people. He knows what God *should* do. And so he is baffled, upset, and perhaps angry that God is *not* doing what God should do.

The rest of Habakkuk's book will continue this argument with God, and God will have some pretty surprising things to say, as well as some challenging and comforting things. In the end, Habakkuk will find himself reassured and restored to his faith in God's sovereign wisdom, even in the midst of the chaos he describes. That's the journey ahead.

However, for the moment we may find ourselves echoing and agreeing with Habakkuk's questions. We find ourselves on the same road as the journey he is on. Perhaps it's even a relief that somebody—somebody actually in the Bible itself!—asks those questions that so trouble our very selves. Again, take heart and read on!

OUR RESPONSE

This whole question of how to justify the character and action (or inaction) of God is sometimes called the issue of "theodicy." If God is righteous, why do the wicked flourish? If God is holy, why does he tolerate the unholy ways of evil people?

Sometimes these theodicy questions just hang around as an intellectual exercise for theologians. However, for Habakkuk and for many of us the whole thing becomes acutely painful. These questions cause deep perplexity as well as a lot of anger. We feel anguish not because we don't care whether God is involved in life here on earth or not, but precisely because *we believe that he is, but cannot see how.*

We feel angry when *human* justice is not done. We are appalled when people commit evil acts and get off with impunity. We protest when nobody is held to account for costly failures, malpractice, or fraud. We despise politicians who lecture us about social ideals and then engage in cronyism, hypocrisy, and corruption. We are furious when negligence, greed, or corruption for short-term profit on the part of big companies cause suffering and death to others—usually the poor and marginalized. We are staggered when one country brutally invades and bombards another, as if we had learned nothing from two world wars. At such times, yes, we feel rightly angry against *human* authorities.

Our struggle feels even more acute when we take the matter to the divine Judge. *He* is supposed to be the God who listens and saves! He is supposed to be the Judge of all the earth who will do what is right (Gen 18:25). So, why does he not? Why are the heavens silent in times like these?

This was Job's question too. Let's see how he seems to take the glowing promises illustrated in Scriptures such as Psalms 145 and 146 and turn them inside out with his questions and observations in Job 24.

Here is what the psalmist celebrates about Yahweh, the Lord God:

> ¹⁴The Lord upholds all who fall
> and lifts up all who are bowed down.
> ¹⁵The eyes of all look to you,
> and you give them their food at the proper time.

¹⁶You open your hand
　　and satisfy the desires of every living thing.

¹⁷The Lord is righteous in all his ways
　　and faithful in all he does.
¹⁸The Lord is near to all who call on him,
　　to all who call on him in truth.
¹⁹He fulfills the desires of those who fear him;
　　he hears their cry and saves them.
²⁰The Lord watches over all who love him,
　　but all the wicked he will destroy. (Ps 145:14–20)

⁷He upholds the cause of the oppressed
　　and gives food to the hungry.
The Lord sets prisoners free,
　　⁸the Lord gives sight to the blind,
the Lord lifts up those who are bowed down,
　　the Lord loves the righteous.
⁹The Lord watches over the foreigner
　　and sustains the fatherless and the widow,
　　but he frustrates the ways of the wicked. (Ps 146:7–9)

Now listen to Job. It sounds like he has just read those psalms
and then looks up, looks around at the world, and says, "No, the
Lord doesn't. Not as far as I can see!"

¹Why does the Almighty not set times for judgment?
　　Why must those who know him look in vain for
　　　　such days?
²There are those who move boundary stones;
　　they pasture flocks they have stolen.
³They drive away the orphan's donkey
　　and take the widow's ox in pledge.
⁴They thrust the needy from the path

and force all the poor of the land into hiding.
⁵Like wild donkeys in the desert,

the poor go about their labor of foraging food;

the wasteland provides food for their children.
⁶They gather fodder in the fields

and glean in the vineyards of the wicked.
⁷Lacking clothes, they spend the night naked;

they have nothing to cover themselves in the cold.
⁸They are drenched by mountain rains

and hug the rocks for lack of shelter.
⁹The fatherless child is snatched from the breast;

the infant of the poor is seized for a debt.
¹⁰Lacking clothes, they go about naked;

they carry the sheaves, but still go hungry.
¹¹They crush olives among the terraces;

they tread the winepresses, yet suffer thirst.
¹²The groans of the dying rise from the city,

and the souls of the wounded cry out for help.

But God charges no one with wrongdoing.

(Job 24:1–12)

Can you see the clashing contradiction between the affirmations of faith in the Psalms and the observations of reality in Job? And the worst of it is that last line: "God charges no one with wrongdoing."

Now, in our next chapter we will begin to hear God's answer to Habakkuk, which is at least in part also an answer to Job—though we'll not be going to that book. This answer will call for a determined exercise of patience and faith, and it will include a vision of God's ultimate purpose for the whole earth.

We, of course, standing on this side of Calvary and the empty tomb, have an even wider perspective from which to address Habakkuk's questions and our own. Yes, we know the great truths of the gospel and the further revelation of Christian faith and hope in the New Testament. But, even with all that, don't we still struggle with questions as we seek to discern the hand of God and the justice of God in the midst of a crazy, violent, and morally bankrupt world?

Habakkuk's "*How long?*" and "*Why?*" are explosive questions that are never far from our minds.

QUESTIONS FOR REFLECTION OR DISCUSSION

1. Do you find it hard, or wrong, to ask difficult questions to God?
2. Have you experienced times of crying out to God, but with no apparent answer? How have you sustained your faith and relationship with God in such times?
3. What aspects of life in our contemporary world would fit the description of Habakkuk 1:3–4?

CHAPTER 2

QUESTIONING GOD'S SOVEREIGNTY: WHEN GOD DOES TAKE ACTION *THROUGH* EVIL PEOPLE

Habakkuk 1:5–17

The world Habakkuk doesn't understand is a world of violence and injustice. It's the world he sees all around him in his own country. For a long time (as it seems from his opening words), Habakkuk has been pouring out his heart to God. He is perplexed, angry, and scared—he protests as he sees all that is going on around him. Is God asleep? Is God impotent? Will God ever answer his complaint? Will God ever do something about it?

At last, as we would expect in a prophetic book, God speaks. And God's first word echoes Habakkuk's own.

GOD'S ANSWER (1:5–11)

Habakkuk had said in verse 3 that he was having to "look" at the injustice all around him in his own nation. And then God answers, "Look a bit wider; look among the *nations*. Not just at your own":

> Look at the nations and watch—
>   and be utterly amazed.
> For I am going to do something in your days
>   that you would not believe,
>   even if you were told. (1:5)

Sometimes God has to tell us to *"look again!"* We can get so absorbed and upset by what we are looking at in our immediate context that we need to step back and take in the wider horizon. We need God's perspective. We need to see that God and the Bible are not only interested in our personal salvation and our immediate intellectual or ethical problems. Rather, there is a *big picture.* There is, in fact, the whole grand narrative of Scripture to take into account, which includes not only God and me but also God and the nations, and even God and the whole creation. Get *that* perspective! Expand your vision!

Martyn Lloyd-Jones makes this point emphatically in his small commentary on Habakkuk. He says that one reason why people have a problem with God's sovereignty in history (as Habakkuk did initially) is that

> . . . there are those who use the Bible in a narrow sense, as being exclusively a text book of personal salvation. Many people seem to think that the sole theme of the Bible is that of man's personal relationship to God. Of course that is one of the central themes, and we thank God for the salvation provided without which we should be left in hopeless despair. But that is not the only theme of the Bible. Indeed, we can go so far as to say that the Bible puts the question of personal salvation into a larger context. Ultimately the main message of the Bible concerns the condition of the entire world and its destiny; and you and I, as individuals, are a part of that larger whole. That is why it starts with the creation of the world rather than of man. The trouble is that we are inclined to be exclusively concerned with our own personal problem, whereas the Bible starts further back: it puts every problem in the context of this world view. . . . Nothing that occurs in history fails to find a place in the divine programme. The great and noble teaching of the

Bible is concerned with the whole question of the world and its destiny.[1]

Thus, God tells Habakkuk to adjust his spectacles and look further. Pay attention to the big picture, the world of nations, and the whole story of God at work in human history.

But far from bringing any comfort, that wider look isn't going to be any better: *"Watch—and be utterly amazed"* (v. 5a). Actually, God's words are a bit stronger than amazement. "You will be astounded and terrified" would be a better expression. *"Brace yourself for a shock"* (MSG).

God Is at Work—but in a Surprising Way (1:5b)

God doesn't expect that Habakkuk will be able immediately to grasp everything God is about to reveal to him. But God *does* want Habakkuk to know that God is *not* inactive. God has not fallen asleep. God is not unaware of the terrible evils going on in Judah. And God is not uncaring, unmoved, or uninterested in them. On the contrary, God has his plans ready and is about to put them into action.

"I am going to do something" is, literally, *"I am working a work* in your days." That is, "I am fully engaged *right now* in these matters." God is on the case already!

Now, this is rather hard for Habakkuk to believe. The events he is witnessing give every appearance that God is absent, whereas God says *he is actually very much present and at work*. In fact, as we now know, God was at work in a way that was going to change things forever for Israel—the destruction of Jerusalem and the Babylonian exile and everything that lay beyond these events.

Well, that was some surprise (and more lay in store)! And,

---

1. Martyn Lloyd-Jones, *From Fear to Faith: Rejoicing in the Lord in Turbulent Times* (1953; repr., Leicester, UK: IVP, 2003), 9.

because God's words were a surprise they would have to be received by *faith*, as God will say in a moment (2:4). Habakkuk will also need *patience* (2:3), for the import of God's words will not be immediately obvious. Indeed, it will be utterly shocking.

Part of the challenge of this book, then, for us readers, is this: are *we* willing—even in principle, as it were—to be amazed by God? Are we willing to accept what we don't find easy to believe? Are we able, by faith in what the Bible says about the sovereignty of God, to perceive and affirm the hand of God in current events, even when those events are horrendous? Habakkuk would not have understood what was happening if God had not revealed it to him, and even then he would find it hard to believe (1:5b). But this is one reason that we have his book in our Bible, warning us that sometimes the work of God in history is surprising, paradoxical, and baffling, and yet still serves God's ultimate sovereign purpose.

The Bible affirms this again and again: God is at work. God is not asleep. God has not forgotten that he is the judge of all the earth. This may well be a world *we* don't understand, but that does not mean it is a world that *God* has abandoned.

But what was God *actually doing* that would leave Habakkuk "*utterly amazed*"? What was this "work" that God was "working" in Habakkuk's day? Was Habakkuk ready for it?

Well, ready or not, God tells him. Try to put yourself in Habakkuk's sandals, listening to what God says next. . . .

God Is Raising Up the Babylonians (1:6–11)

> ⁶*I am raising up the Babylonians,*
> *that ruthless and impetuous people,*
> *who sweep across the whole earth*
> *to seize dwellings not their own.*
> ⁷*They are a feared and dreaded people;*
> *they are a law to themselves*
> *and promote their own honor.*
> ⁸*Their horses are swifter than leopards,*

fiercer than wolves at dusk.
Their cavalry gallops headlong;
    their horsemen come from afar.
They fly like an eagle swooping to devour;
    ⁹they all come intent on violence.
Their hordes advance like a desert wind
    and gather prisoners like sand.
¹⁰They mock kings
    and scoff at rulers.
They laugh at all fortified cities;
    by building earthen ramps they capture them.
¹¹Then they sweep past like the wind and go on—
    guilty people, whose own strength is their god.
        (1:6–11)

"The Babylonians" (NIV) is the same as "the Chaldeans" (ESV, etc). They were originally a rather small people in the south of Mesopotamia, in what we would now call southern Iraq. They suddenly emerged towards the end of the seventh century BC and started an energetic push northward into the heartlands of the old Assyrian Empire. Led by their king Nabopolassar, and then his son Nebuchadnezzar, they captured Nineveh (the capital city of Assyria) in 612 BC. This was the beginning of what is now known as the Neo-Babylonian Empire.

These events must have been well-known in Judah. They would have been an anxious talking point in the streets of Jerusalem. Who are these people? Why have they emerged and conquered the powerful Assyrian Empire so quickly? Where are they going to go next? How can we resist them, or should we try to strike a deal with them? After nearly a hundred and fifty years of living under the heel of Assyria, what will it mean if these Babylonians rise to regional dominance? What kind of people and what kind of empire will they be?

God answers those questions, and Habakkuk's, with a simple,

stark affirmation. He begins with an emphatic exclamation that the NIV omits (1:6):

> *Look, it's me!*
> *I am the one raising up the Babylonians!*

God knows exactly what kind of people they are and how they will behave. So he gives Habakkuk a rapid-fire catalogue of the speed and power of this Babylonian menace. It is a frightening fourfold picture. Remember—this is God describing those God himself is raising up!

a) Ruthless Speed and Conquest (1:6)

The Babylonians are *"ruthless and impetuous."* Merciless in their expansion, they move fast and take everybody by surprise. They *"sweep across the whole earth to seize dwellings not their own."* This is the essence of voracious expansion—just go and take. And do it fast. March in, take over, seize control, conquer, exploit, and steal.

Other empires have boasted of such practices down through the ages. Here are several examples:

- Alexander the Great conquered the sprawling Persian Empire like a hot knife through butter with astonishing speed, slicing through from Greece until he reached the borders of India.
- Julius Caesar famously boasted, "Veni, Vidi, Vici" ("I came, I saw, I conquered") after winning a battle against a kingdom in Asia Minor (northern Turkey) in 47 BC.
- The British took rather longer in Africa and India, but the long-term effects were the same—a great deal of taking, with ruthlessness when necessary.
- Adolf Hitler's rapid expansion put other European nations on the wrong foot and led up to the Second World War.
- Think of how quickly the USA invaded and overran Iraq in 2003—and what profits some companies made from that.

- Remember how surprised the West was when Russia just walked in and annexed Crimea from Ukraine in 2014, and then launched a full-scale invasion in 2022.
- Even more so, remember the shock when ISIS burst out and overran northern Syria and Iraq.
- Think of the tragic historic irony in the rapid return of the Taliban as it took complete control of Afghanistan again.

Some of these conquests have been reversed, but often at great cost. This would also be true for Babylon in the end, as God knew. And the eventual fall of Babylon would be the outcome of the "Woes" that God himself would pronounce against it through Habakkuk (in ch. 2) and Jeremiah. But this realization will not decrease the pain for Habakkuk and Judah as they face this initial terrifyingly fast onslaught. God seemed to be removing one empire (Assyria) only to replace it with another (Babylon) that would conquer at breakneck speed.

b) Unaccountable "Exceptionalism" and Self-Interest (1:7)

Verse 7 is pointed and revealing. Here is how it stands in the Hebrew (the "he" is singular, meaning the king of Babylon and his empire):

> *Terrifying and feared is he;*
> *from himself his law and his sovereignty go forth.*

What that means is: *he makes his own rules and promotes his own greatness.* He is so terrifying because he is a law unto himself and generates his own sovereignty. He accepts no accountability to any norms or standards other than whatever benefits himself and his kingdom. No Geneva Convention is going to restrain his violence and greed. All his decisions and actions flow from himself and for himself.

Characterized in this way, the Babylonians were self-exalting and self-justifying. "Justice" was whatever *they* decided. "Honour, dignity, majesty"—these were simply whatever made *them* great.

When countries begin to believe their own propaganda or to relish how much the rest of the world either admires or fears them (preferably both), they easily fall into a kind of "exceptionalism." That is the belief (which then becomes embedded in actual foreign policy) that the ordinary rules of international behaviour don't apply to us. We must follow our own interests and put ourselves first. International cooperation is for fools and wimps; national self-interest is the only policy that counts. This fuelled the "Make America Great Again" slogan and passion.

Now, of course, it is the proper responsibility of any government to look after its own citizens, protect their security and care for their welfare, and cherish the values and achievements of its own national culture. But when this spills over into national selfishness at the cost of other, poorer nations or into mockery or rejection of all forms of international agreements and collaboration, then it ends up as arrogant national idolatry, a collective amplification of the toxic idolatry of the self.

Here, for example, is how one American commentator criticizes US exceptionalism (which just happens to be a modern form of exceptionalism; the British Empire had many of the same features, still raucously celebrated in the song—so pathetically anachronistic—"Rule, Britannia!"):

> What we're dealing with is not just valuing the United States, but also devaluing the rest of the world—and not just as observers, but as people who believe they have the right, if not the duty, to impose their will on the rest of the world. Exceptionalism is an attitude that tends to include arrogance, ignorance, and aggression, and these tend to do a great deal of damage. . . .
>
> US exceptionalism does not just devalue the individual lives of others. It also devalues the earth as a whole. US

policy is generally not shaped by concern for its impact on the planet's environment. And the attitude of constant competition for the most growth on a finite planet is destructive and ultimately self-defeating. As an exceptionalist—or, as the US government would call the same attitude in someone else, a rogue—the United States keeps itself out of more international treaties than do its peers. It also keeps itself out of the jurisdiction of courts of international law and arbitration. This position hurts the US public, by denying it new developments in human rights. And it deals a severe blow to the rule of law elsewhere, because of the prominence and power of the world's leading rogue nation.[2]

c) Arrogant Military Superiority (1:8–10)

Verses 8–10 portray a militarized nation, a nation that boasts of having superior weaponry that can overrun any enemy. Babylon has the ancient equivalent of fast-moving tanks and armoured vehicles ("horses," "cavalry"). They speed across the terrain like leopards or eagles, which are both fast-moving predators. Modern airpower carries a similar image.

Furthermore, "*They all come intent on* **violence**" (v. 9a; my emphasis; there's that word again). All this military hardware is not for national self-defence, but for ruthless and deliberate conquest. There is something ironic about God echoing Habakkuk here. Habakkuk had cried out "*Violence!*" (v. 2), but God says, "Yes, and you haven't seen the worst of it yet."

God had promised that the descendants of Abraham would multiply like "sand" (Gen 22:17), but in verse 9b sand becomes a picture of a very different kind of multiplication: prisoners, refugees from war, internally displaced peoples, whole nations

---

2. David Swanson, "The Hubris of American Exceptionalism Devalues the Rest of the World," *Truthout*, May 10, 2018, https://truthout.org/articles/the-hubris-of-american -exceptionalism-devalues-the-rest-of-the-world/.

fleeing genocide . . . the world is awash with the casualties of human violence.

And all the while, Babylon's propaganda machine is hard at work, pumping out the background music of arrogant national pride. Other nations are nothing but targets for derision, scoffing, and laughter (v. 10). "I've got a bigger nuclear button than yours. . . ."[3]

d) National Idolatry (1:11)

On and on the Babylonians go, apparently invincible and unstoppable. Until they crash into God's verdict. God has the last word—as he always does and always will. It comes in verse 11b (literal translation):

> *Guilty he is; for this: his own strength is his god.*

Here is a king (Nebuchadnezzar in this case, but it could be any ruler, president, prime minister . . .) who not only boasts of his strength, but also worships it. His own power has reached divine status in his own eyes. This is the idolatry of narcissistic self-importance combined with the idolatry of national pride and power. It is a classic combination that didn't start with Nebuchadnezzar and certainly didn't end with him. "Babylon First!" "Make Babylon Great Again" (there had been an earlier age of Babylonian power in the time of Hammurabi, even before Abraham; Nebuchadnezzar built the *Neo*-Babylonian Empire).

Self-deification—this is the mammoth arrogance and the man-made idolatry that can afflict individuals, but easily becomes the trademark of nations that seek to dominate the world around them for their own benefit. We assume that our success in conquering

---

3. Cf. Donald Trump mocking Kim Jong Un of North Korea; Scott Neuman, "Trump Taunts Kim: My 'Nuclear Button' Is 'Much Bigger' Than Yours," *The Two-Way* (blog), NPR, January 3, 2018, https://www.npr.org/sections/thetwo-way/2018/01/03/575240956/trump-taunts-kim-my-nuclear-button-is-much-bigger-than-yours.

continents gives us some kind of divine right to have done so in the first place. We may still, of course, have symbols, songs, and ceremonies that purport to give glory to God. However, the name and "idea" of God has instead morphed into the national identity, national glorification, and national self-interest of our country. I would see a large element of this in the British Empire and in the way its legacy still resonates in the culture wars in the UK over what really makes modern Britain "Great."

This self-glorifying, self-deifying tendency is what marks the Babylonians out for judgment. Above all the other crimes against humanity (that we'll come to in chapter 2), it is what makes them "*guilty*" before the living God. The Babylonians have become their own god, even though they certainly had other gods with names such as Bel, Nebo, Marduk, and others. But these were simply personifications of the power and glory of the city, the state, the king, and the empire of Babylon. Think of Nebuchadnezzar's gleaming pillar of gold in Daniel 3. It symbolized his state and its power. And everybody must bow down and worship this statue—or face the fiery furnace. Bow or burn. Toast the state, or toast yourself.

It is not surprising, then, that "Babylon" becomes the biblical code word for blasphemous human empires in any and every age. "Babylon" can stand for any arrogant human power that exalts itself and seeks to dominate by military or economic means—or both. There have been plenty of ancient and modern and contemporary "Babylons" in human history. The book of Revelation definitively portrays Babylon's ultimate satanic nature—and its ultimate destiny.

So, Habakkuk 1:6–11 leaves us in no doubt whatsoever: the Babylonians are indeed rapidly emerging as a violent, destructive, rapacious, idolatrous, arrogant, and guilty regional power. *God himself says so.* God is not fooled or naïve. God knows full well what kind of nation this is. God has seen this all before. The Babylonians will certainly follow the Assyrians, and God had put up with that previous empire for a hundred and fifty years. So God knows what

Nebuchadnezzar and his troops have already done over there in Mesopotamia, and God knows what they are likely to go on doing (for just as long as he permits).

But *"I am raising up the Babylonians"* (v. 6), says God. How surprising, how appalling, and how hard to swallow is that?

Let's return to Habakkuk. Picture him there, listening with increasing horror to what God has just told him. You mean, *this* is God's answer to his complaint about the violence and injustice of Judah?! What kind of an answer is that?

HABAKKUK'S STRUGGLE (1:12–2:1)

I imagine there was a rather long silence between 1:11 and 1:12!

Habakkuk digested what God had said to him and let the shock sink in.

But I also imagine a silence in which he pondered the implications and began (only just began) to "get it."

Habakkuk's next words, after all, are initially very affirmative and full of faith and acceptance. He still has agonizing questions in mind, and will ask them in a moment. But he can see what God means, and (at least in part) it seems sensible for him to grasp. There is still another kind of not-so-good-sense-at-all vibe that Habakkuk finds very hard to grasp. But let's at least give full weight to his opening words in response—words that probably came out of some long and deep thought.

What Habakkuk Affirms (1:12a)

> LORD, are you not from everlasting?
>   My God, my Holy One, you will never die. (1:12a)

The last word of verse 11 is *"their* god" (my italics)—the self-made god of the Babylonians. Here, by stark and impressive contrast, Habakkuk begins his response by affirming who *his* God is. *"My* God . . ." (my italics), he exclaims. Habakkuk's God is not just some jumped-up god of recent imperial expansions in the Middle East, but *the God who has been there from all eternity.* And he names his God—the LORD, Yahweh, the covenant name of the God of Israel who had proved his faithfulness to his people through many centuries.

"Are you not from everlasting?" This is a rhetorical question, which of course expects the answer "Yes!" It echoes the faith that Habakkuk shared with all the generations of his people—the faith that breathes through their stories and their worship:

> The eternal God is your refuge,
>> and underneath are the everlasting arms.
>>> (Deut 33:27)

> ¹Lord, you have been our dwelling place
>> throughout all generations.
> ²Before the mountains were born
>> or you brought forth the whole world,
>>> from everlasting to everlasting you are God. (Ps 90:1–2)

But this everlasting God is not some distant deity known only in history and song. No—Habakkuk affirms his personal relationship with Yahweh three times: *"My* God, *my* Holy One. . . . *my* Rock (v. 12; my italics)."

"My Holy One" means the God who is distinctive from all other so-called gods. Often in Israelite worship the rhetorical question is asked, "Who is like the LORD?"—the expected answer, of course, being "No one." Yahweh has no rivals or competitors in power, majesty, justice, salvation, grace, forgiveness, revelation, guidance, and instruction . . . and all the other vast affirmations the Scriptures make about him. Habakkuk knows who the living God is, and he knows there is no other god like him. In fact, there is no other god at all!

"My Rock." "The Rock" is one of the oldest metaphors for the

God of Israel. This moniker goes back to Moses, who uses it in his great song at the end of Deuteronomy:

> ³I will proclaim the name of the LORD.
>   Oh, praise the greatness of our God!
> ⁴He is the Rock, his works are perfect,
>   and all his ways are just.
> A faithful God who does no wrong,
>   upright and just is he. (Deut 32:3–4)

This picture speaks of security. Compared with a swamp or a dangerous river, a massive rock is a safe place to stand. Or the rock may be a great overhanging crag which is safe to shelter under from a storm. God, the Rock, is *dependable*. You can stand on his word; you can trust in his protection and be safe.

So, since Yahweh the Rock God is still there, and has been there longer than any earthly rock or mountain, then there is only one conclusion:

"You will never die" (v. 12a NIV 2011). Or, perhaps better, "**we will not die**" (NIV 1973; my emphasis; there is a slight variation in the manuscript evidence). But, either way, whether Habakkuk is talking about God's eternity or his people's security, this is a statement of confident faith. Yahweh lives and *he* will not die. Therefore *we*, the people belonging to Yahweh, will not perish either, no matter how violent and powerful the Babylonians may be, and no matter how many individual people may suffer and die if they attack us. God's people will not be destroyed.

We can be sure of this. This is not The End of the story, for it is not the end of the God whose story it is. God's people will survive, for the Babylonians and "their god" cannot defeat or destroy the living and eternal God, the Holy One of Israel. And in God's eternity lies his people's security.

So, this is what Habakkuk affirms, and it is a good starting point and a very solid rock to stand on. But then he goes further.

What Habakkuk Accepts (1:12b)

> *You, LORD, have appointed them to execute judgment;*
> *you, my Rock, have ordained them to punish. (1:12b)*

At this point Habakkuk perceives and puts into his own words what God had not quite explicitly said. But this is where his train of thought, coupled with God's words, has led.

Remember, back in verses 2–4 Habakkuk had asked why God was not acting in judgment on the wicked people in Judah: *"Justice never prevails . . . justice is perverted"* (v. 4). Surely the God of justice ought to be doing something about this! Well, now God has answered that complaint by saying that he is raising up the Babylonians. So, the implication must be that God is doing this in order to use the Babylonians as the agent through whom God will execute his just judgment on Judah, that is, *on God's own people!* God *is* doing justice, but not quite as Habakkuk would have wanted.

Nevertheless, Habakkuk accepts this conclusion. He states it quite emphatically with no ambiguity. His words in verse 12b echo his complaint in verse 4. The words "justice" and "judgment" are the same word in Hebrew (*mishpat*). In Judah, "justice" (*mishpat*) was being denied or perverted. But now God has appointed "them" (the Babylonians) "for justice" (*mishpat*; NIV "to execute judgment"; ESV "as a judgment"). Habakkuk then explains exactly what he means, in the last line of the verse: *"You, my Rock, have ordained them to punish."* The Babylonians will be the instrument of God's retributive justice.

Can we see the progression and the shift in thinking that is going on here?

- In verses 3–4 Habakkuk complained that God is *not* doing justice.
- In verse 12 Habakkuk accepts that God *is* doing justice but doing it through the Babylonians.

So, then, the primary point which Habakkuk can accept, and indeed was longing for, is that *God is indeed going to act in judgment* on the evildoers in Judah. God is going to "do justice" by bringing on them the stipulated curses of the covenant. They would reap the reward of their evil behaviour. That much is what the Israelites knew from the Torah, from the words of other prophets, and indeed from their own history over many centuries (as can be seen in the book of Judges). Persistent and unrepented sin inevitably brings God's judgment. Habakkuk knew and accepted as much. The "Judge of all the earth" would indeed do justice. Evil would not have the last word.

But here's the thing that was much harder to accept. It was this idea that "*you . . . have ordained* **them**" (v. 12b; my emphasis).

Them!

This horrifically violent foreign enemy, this wicked, arrogant, greedy, destructive, self-worshiping, god-manufacturing, pagan empire! That's how God himself describes them. And God intends to use *them* as the tool of his justice?

How can God do this?

This leads Habakkuk into his second round of protest and questioning. And so we move from Habakkuk affirming and accepting to Habakkuk arguing (again!).

But do notice this, however. The argument from verse 13 to the end of chapter 1 comes *after* the affirmations of verse 12. Habakkuk has got his perspective right. Of course he still has his questions. Of course there are things he cannot understand. But all his questioning takes place on the foundation of biblical faith. He raises issues that *he cannot understand* on the basis of what *he knows to be true* about God and the ways of God. Indeed, it is precisely *because* of what Habakkuk believes about God that his questions arise.

There is some similarity here with Qoheleth in the book of Ecclesiastes. Like Qoheleth:

- Habakkuk is utterly convinced of his faith in God, but he cannot *deny* the problem he faces.
- What Habakkuk does not do (as Qoheleth also did not) is to abandon his faith in God simply because he cannot *understand* the problem.

Here is how David Prior puts it:

Habakkuk has become free to remonstrate with God at this level only after planting his feet firmly on the *Rock*, on God's eternal changelessness and on his personal commitment in a covenantal relationship between God and the prophet. . . . There has always been this important distinction between bitter cynicism and believing confrontation: *one is a denial that refuses to believe, the other is a belief that refuses to deny*; one makes assertions and will not stay for an answer, the other makes assertions and will not move until there is an answer.[4]

And so, on this foundation, we move on with Habakkuk to his second big question to God.

What Habakkuk Argues (1:13–2:1)

> [13] *Your eyes are too pure to look on evil;*
>   *you cannot tolerate wrongdoing.*
> *Why then do you tolerate the treacherous?*
>   *Why are you silent while the wicked*
>   *swallow up those more righteous than themselves?*
> [14] *You have made people like the fish in the sea,*
>   *like the sea creatures that have no ruler.*
> [15] *The wicked foe pulls all of them up with hooks,*
>   *he catches them in his net,*

---

4. David Prior, *The Message of Joel, Micah and Habakkuk*, The Bible Speaks Today (Leicester, UK: IVP, 1998), 222–23 (my italics).

> *he gathers them up in his dragnet;*
>   *and so he rejoices and is glad.*
> *[16] Therefore he sacrifices to his net*
>   *and burns incense to his dragnet,*
> *for by his net he lives in luxury*
>   *and enjoys the choicest food.*
> *[17] Is he to keep on emptying his net,*
>   *destroying nations without mercy?*
> *[2:1] I will stand at my watch*
>   *and station myself on the ramparts;*
> *I will look to see what he will say to me,*
>   *and what answer I am to give to this complaint.*
>   (1:13–2:1)

In verse 13 Habakkuk recalls the problem he had in verse 3; it has unfortunately expanded alarmingly. Back in verse 3 his complaining question was, "*Why do you make* **me** *look at injustice?*" (my emphasis). Now, it seems that he is saying, "It's bad enough that *I* have to do so. I'm a sinner like the rest of the human race. My eyes are used to seeing evil every day. But *you, LORD!* You are the God of ultimate holiness. '*Your eyes are too pure to look on evil.*' So, '*why do* **you** *idly look at traitors*' (v. 13 ESV; my emphasis)? And, apparently, you not only look at them, but make use of them to accomplish your purpose. How can you possibly do this, God?"

Why (v. 3)? *Why* (v. 13)? The question just won't lie down.

Habakkuk is struggling with the apparent contradiction between God's pure holiness on the one hand and God's involvement with wicked people on the other hand, especially if God plans to use such unjust humans as agents of his justice.

Habakkuk would have known what the psalmists say so clearly in many places; things like this, for example:

> [4] For you are not a God who is pleased with wickedness;
>   with you, evil people are not welcome.

> ⁵The arrogant cannot stand
>> in your presence.
> You hate all who do wrong;
>> ⁶you destroy those who tell lies.
> The bloodthirsty and deceitful
>> you, LORD, detest. (Ps 5:4–6)

Yet here is this same God announcing that he will use precisely such people to achieve his purposes in history.

Now, at this point Habakkuk makes a move that is very typical of us humans; he claims the moral high ground! That's where he goes in the second half of verse 13:

> *Why are you silent while the wicked*
> *swallow up* **those more righteous than themselves***?*
> *(1:13b; my emphasis)*

Habakkuk is referring to the Babylonians invading Judah. But what he means is: "God, I know that we, the people of Judah, are bad in all the ways I listed in verses 3–4. I accept that we deserve your judgment. But surely you can see that *we're not as bad as they are*—those Babylonians! So how can you punish some people who are *bad* (us) by using other people who are even *worse* (them)?!"

Rather, like Job and so many others, Habakkuk wants to take over from God the role of moral judge of the universe. It's the kind of self-confidence that wants to say, "If I ruled the world . . . I'd do things very differently." But the fact is, of course, that God doesn't do league tables of sin. Nor is God bound to use as agents of judgment only those whom *we* have vetted and approved.

Yes, the Bible does show us that some acts of wickedness are worse than others, and God's judgment undoubtedly takes this into account. But the reality is, "all have sinned . . ." (Rom 3:23). Or, as another psalm puts it:

^{2}The LORD looks down from heaven
   on all mankind
to see if there are any who understand,
   any who seek God.
^{3}All have turned away, all have become corrupt;
   there is no one who does good,
   not even one.
                (Ps 14:2–3, quoted by Paul in Rom 3:10–12)

God has the prerogative to exercise his justice in whatever way he chooses. It is not a case of only using the righteous to punish the wicked—especially since in God's scales there are no people or nations so righteous that they do not deserve judgment themselves (a point God made to Israel very firmly in Deuteronomy 9).

Nevertheless, Habakkuk presses his argument in verses 14–17. He compares human beings to fish in the sea. There we all are, swimming around happily together. But then along comes the fisherman with his net (not just an angler with a line and hook for one fish at a time, but a whole net to capture shoals at a time). He drags us up in his conquering greed, treating humans like mere floundering fish, and then boasts of his catch.

This is a very graphic picture of what warring empires do to whole populations. It makes us think of the horrors of slave trading, genocide, ethnic cleansing, and human trafficking. All of these atrocities are hugely profitable to those who benefit from them and finance their obscenely luxurious lifestyle, paid for in human misery (v. 16b).

So, Habakkuk pictures the Babylonians worshiping their "net" (v. 16), that is, the military might that enables them to sweep up whole populations into their great imperial machine for their own profit and glory. They deify the whole system because the justification for their wickedness and violence is simple: it works! It makes us rich! Every self-enriching empire in history has found ways to justify (and even sanctify) its methods, since the results are so gratifying. You can find plenty of religious reasons to justify your actions when it turns out to be massively profitable for yourself—or your company, or your country, or empire.

Will this monstrous evil go on forever (v. 17)? Habakkuk cannot silence these questions. And, surely, he speaks for us as we agonize over the same things in this world which we can't understand, governed by the God we are also struggling to understand.

Why (v. 13)?

How long (v. 17)?

Habakkuk persists, doesn't he?

Let's summarize what we have seen in this chapter:

- God has expanded Habakkuk's vision, calling him to think about the wider international scene over which God rules, not just what was happening in his own country (v. 5a).
- God has told Habakkuk that God is at work in history, not only in the past but in the worrying present and the very near future (v. 5b).
- God says that he is raising up the Babylonians, and Habakkuk perceives that God intends to use them as the agent of his judgment (vv. 6, 12).

But for Habakkuk, God's reply only *amplifies his problem.* It was problem enough that God should allow the wicked among *Israel* to get away for so long without God acting. It was already hard to cope with the silence and inaction of God (vv. 2–4).

But it is now an *even bigger problem* that God should actively raise up and use an even more wicked nation to *do* justice against his own people. It is hard to understand the *action* of God when the agent of God's justice is itself so manifestly wicked! (vv. 12–17).

- It's a problem when God doesn't do justice!
- It's a problem when God does do justice!

Well, Habakkuk has lodged his second questioning protest. And now he expects a long wait—but he is prepared for that. He doesn't expect a quick-fix answer, and neither should we.

> *I will stand at my watch*
> *   and station myself on the ramparts;*
> *I will look to see what he will say to me,*
> *   and what answer I am to give to this complaint. (2:1)*

He positions himself like a watchman, a lonely sentry on the city walls, waiting and watching all night long. He needs an answer from God, but he also needs to know how he is to answer his own "complaint"—presumably to others who ask the same thing. In our next chapter, we shall hear the response that God eventually gives.

QUESTIONS FOR REFLECTION OR DISCUSSION

1. Have there been times when you were concerned about a particular local or national issue, and then found it important to take a wider perspective of all that God is doing in the world?
2. Do you think we still have a tendency to divide the world into "good guys and bad guys," or perhaps into "bad guys and even worse guys"? Does Habakkuk help us recognize the danger of such a simplistic morality?
3. How patient do we have to be sometimes to discern how and where God is already at work in a situation where we think that everything is utterly and only bad in every way?

CHAPTER 3

LIVING BY FAITH

Habakkuk 2:1–4

In our last two chapters we have seen how Habakkuk doesn't like it when God is silent in the face of wicked people. And he doesn't like it when God plans to use even more wicked people (in his view) as agents of judgment. He has laid both questions before God, and is now waiting patiently for an answer:

> I will stand at my watch
>> and station myself on the ramparts;
> I will look to see what he will say to me,
>> and what answer I am to give to this complaint. (2:1)

God's second answer comes in two parts. It begins with a general statement in 2:2–4, and then moves on to a much more detailed verdict on Babylon in 2:5–20, which we'll cover in our next chapter. That catalogue of "Woes" at one level merely confirms Habakkuk's worst fears (Babylon is even worse than he thought), and yet gives him the strange reassurance that God is perfectly aware of Babylon's evils and has already marked *them* out for judgment. God is not blind; Habakkuk is not pointing out something God hadn't noticed.

A WORD FOR ALL THE WORLD (2:2)

We don't know how long Habakkuk had to wait for God's second answer, but at last it comes. And the first thing God tells him is that the revelation God is about to give him will not be for him alone:

> *Write down the revelation*
> *and make it plain on tablets*
> *so that a herald may run with it. (2:2)*

Habakkuk is to write down what God reveals to him, on tablets (to be durable) so that it can be read and announced by a herald ("one who runs"). Whatever God tells Habakkuk, Habakkuk must tell the world. *Everybody needs to hear this!*

That is why we have this book of Habakkuk in our Bibles today. Whether Habakkuk literally wrote God's word on clay tablets or (more probably) that this was simply a figure of speech for making sure the word of God was written down in a durable way that could not be tampered with—he did write it down! And this word, the book of Habakkuk, has survived because God has providentially preserved those writings that he wanted to be included in the canon of Holy Scripture.

What follows, then, was certainly a word for Habakkuk himself in answer to his personal agonized questions. But it is also a word for us who read his words centuries later. And, indeed, it is a word for the world! When God speaks, "*let* **all the earth** *be silent*" and listen (2:20; my emphasis). We are justified, then, in listening in on Habakkuk's conversation with God, trying hard as we do so to hear God's truth for ourselves and our own day.

A CALL FOR CONFIDENT PATIENCE (2:3)

The second thing that God says to Habakkuk, for all of us to hear, is rather anticlimactic, it would seem. "Wait for it," says God, "Be patient . . .":

> *For the revelation awaits an appointed time;*
> *it speaks of the end*
> *and will not prove false.*

Though it linger, wait for it;
    it will certainly come
    and will not delay. (2:3)

And we can surely hear Habakkuk thinking, "But, Lord, don't you think I've waited long enough already? That's the whole point. Remember my very first words to you? *'How long . . . ?'*" (1:2).

But God insists. What he is about to reveal may take a long time before it all takes place, but "*it will certainly come.*" God's sovereign purpose in history will be accomplished. God will not "*prove false.*" That's because God does not tell lies, and his word will always accomplish what God sends it to do (Isa 55:10–11).

In our next chapter, we shall see something of what that waiting will mean. Habakkuk 2:5–20 covers a significant stretch of time. It spans from the "Woes" that await those who trample the earth and its peoples (starting with the Babylonians themselves) all the way until the time when the whole earth "*will be filled with the knowledge of the glory of the LORD*" (2:14).

Two and a half thousand years after God said these words to Habakkuk, we are still not there on that glory-filled earth. Thus, Habakkuk 2:14 is a glorious prospect we, too, can look forward to. It lay in Habakkuk's future, and it still lies in ours.

So, there is a vision in chapter 2 that moves from Babylon in Habakkuk's day to a global message of divine judgment and ultimate purpose for the whole earth. And God says, to us as much as to Habakkuk: "Trust God and be patient. It will come. For *God himself* will come."

Now Habakkuk knew about God's imminent action—or should have known. Israel's worship resonates with this kind of patient expectation that God will ultimately act to put all things right—to judge the wicked and vindicate the righteous. Take a look, for example, at Psalm 34 or Psalm 75. Or join in this affirmation of corporate hope:

²⁰We wait in hope for the LORD;
>   he is our help and our shield.
²¹In him our hearts rejoice,
>   for we trust in his holy name.
²²May your unfailing love be with us, LORD,
>   even as we put our hope in you. (Ps 33:20–22)

On an even grander scale, we can also join even now in the songs of all nations and all creation, in anticipation of God coming to put things right once and for all. For when God acts in ultimate justice, then there will be stability, righteousness, and rejoicing.

¹⁰Say among the nations, "The LORD reigns."
>   The world is firmly established, it cannot be moved;
>   he will judge the peoples with equity.

¹¹Let the heavens rejoice, let the earth be glad;
>   let the sea resound, and all that is in it.
¹²Let the fields be jubilant, and everything in them;
>   let all the trees of the forest sing for joy.
¹³Let all creation rejoice before the LORD, for he comes,
>   he comes to judge the earth.
He will judge the world in righteousness
>   and the peoples in his faithfulness.
>   (Ps 96:10–13)

The New Testament also reissues this future vision as a message for us. We have "hope" (in the full biblical sense of confident assurance) that the future is in God's hands. God has already won the decisive victory over the powers of evil through the life, death, and resurrection of Jesus Christ. And God will conclusively finish the war when Christ returns. There will be the final judgment in which God will put all things right, and then the new creation in

which God will make all things new. That is the great future that
awaits us as we wait for it—or, rather, as we wait for God. This is
a "waiting" that we share with creation itself. As Paul put it (notice
how many times he uses the word "wait"):

> [18]I consider that our present sufferings are not worth com-
> paring with the glory that will be revealed in us. [19]For the
> creation *waits* in eager expectation for the children of God
> to be revealed. [20]For the creation was subjected to frustra-
> tion, not by its own choice, but by the will of the one who
> subjected it, in hope [21]that the creation itself will be liberated
> from its bondage to decay and brought into the freedom and
> glory of the children of God.
>
> [22]We know that the whole creation has been groaning
> as in the pains of childbirth right up to the present time.
> [23]Not only so, but we ourselves, who have the firstfruits of
> the Spirit, groan inwardly as we *wait* eagerly for our adoption
> to sonship, the redemption of our bodies. [24]For in this hope
> we were saved. But hope that is seen is no hope at all. Who
> hopes for what they already have? [25]But if we hope for what
> we do not yet have, we *wait* for it patiently. (Rom 8:18–25;
> my italics)

This is why Paul prays that believers should be strengthened
for endurance and patience. Christian faith is for the long haul,
not the quick sprint:

> [Be] strengthened with all power according to his glorious
> might so that you may have great endurance and patience.
> (Col 1:11)

And just in case we think two thousand years is really a bit
too long to be kept waiting, Peter urges us to adjust our clocks to
God's time scale:

[8]But do not forget this one thing, dear friends: With the Lord a day is like a thousand years, and a thousand years are like a day. [9]The Lord is not slow in keeping his promise, as some understand slowness. Instead he is patient with you, not wanting anyone to perish, but everyone to come to repentance. (2 Pet 3:8–9)

If God himself is patient, we also can be. Faith is proved real in the waiting.

A FUNDAMENTAL DIVIDE (2:4)

The third thing God says to Habakkuk sets out a very stark distinction. Here is a dichotomy that runs through the whole human race. Indeed, it ran through Israel in Habakkuk's day, and it runs through the whole Bible from Genesis 3 to Revelation 20:

> *Behold, his soul is puffed up; it is not upright within him,*
> *but the righteous shall live by his faith. (2:4 ESV)*

This verse forms a kind of preface to all that God will say next. Here is what determines God's verdict—not only on the Babylonians (though they are the immediate target), but on all people. Here is the fundamental divide between two kinds of people:

- There are those who are puffed up and proud, whose whole inner person (their soul) is not right at all.
- There are also those who are in a right relationship with God because they are living in faith and faithfulness.

God will immediately go on to expand on the first category of people in a scorching condemnation of Babylon (vv. 5–19). And in chapter three Habakkuk will help us understand what it means (and costs) to be among the second category.

Let's look at the summary statements in 2:4. As I said, this verse stands like an introduction to all that follows.

The Proud (2:4a)

The Hebrew of the first half of verse 4 is difficult. It reads very bluntly: "swollen (or puffed up), not upright is his 'soul' within him." The word "soul" is not very good as a translation of the Hebrew *nephesh*, which means the living person, "me as I am in myself," with all my intentions, desires, and emotions. This first half of the verse seems to speak of the arrogance of human hearts—an arrogance that drives us towards decisions, words, and actions that are "*not upright*," that is, they are out of line with the way God wants human life to flourish. This, we might say, is the "normal" human life ever since the fall. We simply do not think, feel, or behave in ways that are "upright," that are morally in tune with the character of God.

Now, the immediate context refers to the Babylonian king and people, as the following verses make clear. But in the wider message that Habakkuk is commissioned to bring (v. 2), it can describe anybody who is not living in faith and obedience to the living God. For such a one, "his puffed-up soul is not upright within him" (my translation). That is, these people are not behaving in a way that is upright, good, and pleasing to God. And they don't care that they aren't. They are too "puffed up" to bother with what God thinks.

To be clear, we should not read that first half of verse 4 as only referring to egregious megalomaniacs like Nebuchadnezzar. There is a deep well of pride and self-sufficiency at the heart of the human condition, a well that feeds the springs of every fallen human heart. This predicament goes right back to the garden in Eden, when human beings chose to distrust God's goodness, disbelieve God's warnings, and disobey God's instruction. Instead, we decided that we would choose for ourselves what is "good and evil." And in that arrogant grasp of moral autonomy, we dethroned God and substituted ourselves as the self-asserting source of all moral authority. Thus, "puffed up" with our own claimed ability, we lost our uprightness and fell into all the consequences of our rebellion and sin.

This is the diagnosis of our fallen human condition, which the rest of the Bible tells us is universal. And this forms the dark backdrop that stands in stark contrast to the second half of verse 4.

The Righteous (2:4b)

Remarkably, this half of the verse consists of just three words in Hebrew, and yet what immense layers of meaning are expressed by them! Here they are in the Hebrew order: each English phrase translates a single word in Hebrew.

- But the righteous person
- through his or her faith (or faithfulness)
- will live.

The word order would allow two possible nuances of meaning, depending on whether the middle word (faith) is taken with the first word (righteous) or with the third word (live). So, here is what happens in either case:

1. The person who is righteous on account of his or her faith will live.
2. The person who is righteous must live by his or her faith (or in faithfulness).

The first may sound more familiar, since it is quoted by Paul in Romans as, "the just shall live by faith" (Rom 1:17 KJV). This is the verse whose "discovery" by Martin Luther in 1515 led to the great Reformation doctrine of justification by faith alone. However, it is probable that the second sense is closer to what God meant Habakkuk to understand, although Abraham would vouch for the first sense, as we shall see in a moment.

Either way (or both), this is God's reassuring answer to
Habakkuk's complaint in 1:13–17. The wicked were swallowing
up the righteous, he complained, and were being allowed to do
so by God's permission and with no end in sight. Would this go
on forever? Would the righteous die out completely, then? NO,
says God, those who are righteous *will live*, not perish. It sounds
very like Psalm 34:15–22. There is life, there is hope, and there is
a future for the righteous. The righteous will not perish but live.

But who are they? Who are "the righteous"?

Let's ask Abraham.

We learn from Abraham that righteousness consists of both
trusting God and *obeying* God. Righteousness is not an abstract
concept or moral state. It is fundamentally a matter of our relationship with God and how we respond to God's words and actions.
After God made his astonishing promises to Abraham, we are told
that Abraham simply (and against all odds) took God at his word:

> Abram believed the LORD, and he credited it to him as
> righteousness. (Gen 15:6)

So that was the *beginning* of his faith-based righteousness, but
not the end of it.

Abraham went on to prove his faith by obeying God's commands on various occasions. God consequently credited that
obedience to him also and built it into the promise. After Abraham
had shown himself willing to sacrifice Isaac, God renewed his
promise, concluding:

> [16]I swear by myself, declares the LORD, that *because you
> have done this* and have not withheld your son, your only
> son, [17]I will surely bless you and make your descendants
> as numerous as the stars in the sky and as the sand on
> the seashore. Your descendants will take possession of the
> cities of their enemies, [18]and through your offspring all

nations on earth will be blessed, *because you have obeyed me*. (Gen 22:16–18; my italics)

Later, God repeated the same reasoning when he renewed the promise to Isaac:

> ⁴. . . and through your offspring all nations on earth will be blessed, ⁵*because Abraham obeyed me* and did everything I required of him, keeping my commands, my decrees and my instructions. (Gen 26:4–5; my italics)

So, then, Abraham's *faith*, the faith that initially put him in a right relationship with God, was proved in Abraham's *obedience* that followed. And that is the right order throughout the whole Bible. First, we put our faith in what God promises, and then we show our faith by obeying what God commands. That was what the apostle Paul was longing to see among all the nations in his very Abrahamic phrase, "the obedience that comes from faith" (Rom 1:5; 16:26).

Later, when God had rescued Abraham's descendants from slavery in the mighty exodus redemption, righteousness for Israel became a matter not only of faith in what God had *promised*, but of responding to what God had actually *done* in their history. God's great act of saving grace called for a response of exclusive faith, worship, and obedience to him alone. That's what it meant to walk in the way of the Lord: by "doing what is right and just"—as God had first told Abraham himself (Gen 18:19). That's who "the righteous" were.

The word "response" is key. God's grace comes first. Our obedience is always in response to grace, not in order to earn grace, or blessing, or anything else.

So, that's how Abraham helps us to answer this question: who are the righteous?

Let's ask Moses as well. Notice what God says to the people of

Israel in the first words he spoke to them when he gathered them
to himself at Mt. Sinai after the exodus:

> ³Then Moses went up to God, and the LORD called to him
> from the mountain and said, "This is what you are to say to
> the descendants of Jacob and what you are to tell the people
> of Israel: ⁴"You yourselves have seen what I did to Egypt, and
> how I carried you on eagles' wings and brought you to myself.
> ⁵Now if you obey me fully and keep my covenant, then out
> of all nations you will be my treasured possession. Although
> the whole earth is mine, ⁶you will be for me a kingdom of
> priests and a holy nation.' These are the words you are to
> speak to the Israelites." (Exod 19:3–6)

Can you see the order and logic? "You have seen what *I* have
done . . . Now, if *you* obey . . . then you will be . . ." God's saving
grace comes first, then responsive obedience is called for, and then
identity, role, and mission in the world are granted.

Righteousness is not mentioned in that short speech by God,
although it is certainly implied: this is how God has *put his people
right* by exercising justice against Egypt on their behalf, and now
this is how God expects them to *live right* in the world as a "holy
nation."

And this is exactly how Moses instructs parents to explain to
their children the whole meaning of their national epic, the story
they were in:

> ²⁰In the future, when your son asks you, "What is the
> meaning of the stipulations, decrees and laws the LORD our
> God has commanded you?" ²¹tell him: "We were slaves of
> Pharaoh in Egypt, but the LORD brought us out of Egypt
> with a mighty hand. ²²Before our eyes the LORD sent signs
> and wonders—great and terrible—on Egypt and Pharaoh
> and his whole household. ²³But he brought us out from there

to bring us in and give us the land he promised on oath to our ancestors. [24]The LORD commanded us to obey all these decrees and to fear the LORD our God, so that we might always prosper and be kept alive, as is the case today. [25]And if we are careful to obey all this law before the LORD our God, as he has commanded us, *that will be our righteousness.*" (Deut 6:20–25; my italics)

It is so important not to take that last verse on its own and turn it into so-called "works righteousness." Moses is *not* saying that righteousness is something the Israelites could earn or deserve through obeying the law. That is a fundamental misunderstanding which, sadly, many people still have in relation to the Old Testament as a whole. But look at the context and the way the conversation runs. The son asks, "What is all this law that we are observing, Dad?" (the question can mean, "What's the point of, or purpose of, or rationale for . . ."). Then the father seeks to answer the question about the meaning and purpose of the *law* by telling the story of *redemption*, the gospel story of the Old Testament—the old, old story of Yahweh and his love. "And because of what God has done for us, we are to respond by obeying him—that's only right, isn't it, son?"

- God delivered us from slavery; that's *God's* righteousness (God acting in justice to put things right for us).
- So we love him (Deut 6:5) and prove our love by obeying him; that's *our* righteousness (our right response to God's saving love).

Back to our question, then: who are the righteous?

For Habakkuk, steeped in the stories and Scriptures and songs of Israel, the righteous are those who have put their faith in the promises of Yahweh God, who remember with thankfulness his redeeming acts in their history (especially the exodus), who have committed themselves to worship Yahweh alone, and who are striving to walk in his ways by covenantal love and obedience. The righteous are people who know that this is the way to remain within the sphere of God's blessing. It is also the way of life itself, even through death, if it comes to that. And the righteous are people who will *go on living in faith and obedience* even in the midst of anxiety, need, opposition, and suffering, waiting in hope for God's promised future. That is the kind of faith-based righteousness which fills the Psalms. It's the kind of righteousness that is so severely put to the test in the book of Job. And, later, it is the kind of scriptural "righteousness in the sight of God" that Luke saw exemplified in Zechariah and Elizabeth (Luke 1:6) and Simeon (Luke 2:25), and even in the gentile Cornelius (Acts 10).

There is one more flavor in the rich texture of these three Hebrew words. That middle word, "by their faith," is the word *'emunah*, which can be translated by both "faith" and "faithfulness." It speaks of both *trusting* and *being trustworthy*. In terms of our relationship with God, then, this word covers both putting our faith *in* God and being faithful *to* God. The person who trusts in God lives out his or her faith by being faithful to God—which includes rejecting any worship of other gods and walking only in the way of the Lord in obedience to his word and will.

With just three words, then, the second half of Habakkuk 2:4 has a depth of meaning and resonance that calls for a lot of expansion. Perhaps we can express it like this:

> *The person who is in a right relationship with God by putting his or her faith in his word, and responding in faith to his saving work, will find true life from God himself. And that person must go on living by faith, both by continuing to trust God for the present and future and by being faithful to God even in the midst of adversity.*

"The righteous, by their faith, shall live."

What immense theological and pastoral freight, and what combined challenge and reassurance, are carried in just three Hebrew words!

Habakkuk is being summoned to be among the righteous, that is, among those of his own people, many or few, who were still seeking to trust in God and be faithful to him in spite of all they saw going on around them. And he is being challenged to *go on trusting God* even when God informs him about the horrendous prospect that lies ahead in the immediate future. Habakkuk is called to go on living by faith in the God who is in sovereign governance of history—including the baffling events of his own time. He needs to go on living by faith in a world he cannot fully understand.

And Habakkuk 2:4 summons us to the same righteous and faithful living.

Indeed, as we read these words that God spoke to Habakkuk from the perspective of our own place in God's story, we have greater grounds for such faith. For we have put our faith in Habakkuk's God as the God who, in the fullness of time, would enter this cruel world. He would take upon himself the worst that human and satanic evil could inflict, through religious hatred and imperial cruelty worse than the Babylonians. God would bear the total weight of such evil in God's own self in the person of God's Son. And in the death and resurrection of Jesus Christ, God would defeat evil, sin, and Satan and emerge victorious over death itself. *That*, the cross and resurrection of God's Son, would be God's climactic answer to Habakkuk's questions—and ours. For God was in Christ reconciling the world—even the world we don't understand—to himself (cf. 2 Cor 5:19).

Because God has done all this in Christ, we, too, are called to live as those who know this truth and believe in him. As we put our trust in God, we know that we are in a right relationship with him, secure in his promise that holds now and for all eternity.

But, more than that, we put our trust in the God whom

we know is "the Judge of all the earth," who will ultimately and irreversibly "do right" (Gen 18:25). We know the story we are in, and we know how the story ends—when Christ returns to put all things right.

We still live in a crazy and agonizing world that we do not understand, which contains all the problems that Habakkuk observed—and worse. But, like him, we are summoned to go on living by faith. This does not mean just our *initial act of faith* through which, by God's grace, we were saved and justified in God's sight, but also our *ongoing daily faith* in the living God. We live as those who confidently trust that, however baffling and painful events may seem to us while we are struggling in the midst of them, God is working out his sovereign purposes. We live in the sure and certain hope that the day will come when "the earth will be filled with the knowledge of the glory of the LORD as the waters cover the sea" (2:14).

QUESTIONS FOR REFLECTION OR DISCUSSION

1. What kind of people (or specific people) in today's world would you describe as "puffed up" in the way Habakkuk describes? Does God view them any differently from those of Habakkuk's day?

2. Does this chapter's analysis of "the righteous," in its scriptural context in the Old Testament, accord with how you think of the righteous today? How might you need to adjust your mental picture of what "righteousness" means in the light of these verses?

3. How has this chapter's discussion of the famous words of Habakkuk 2:4 modified, enriched, or amplified your interpretation of Paul's quotation of this verse in Romans 1:17?

DECLARING GOD'S JUDGMENT: FIVE MARKS OF SOCIAL EVIL

Habakkuk 2:5–20

Habakkuk had protested to God that the Babylonians were an evil empire (1:13–17). And God agrees! They are, indeed! Habakkuk 2:5 expresses exactly that:

> *Indeed, wine betrays him;*
>> *he is arrogant and never at rest.*
> *Because he is as greedy as the grave*
>> *and like death is never satisfied,*
> *he gathers to himself all the nations*
>> *and takes captive all the peoples.*

In verse 5 and through the rest of this chapter, "*he*" and "*him*" refer to the king of Babylon, Nebuchadnezzar, as we learn elsewhere. Or it may be a kind of personification of the whole Babylonian Empire that was fearsomely on the rise in Habakkuk's day. The Babylonians are drunk with power and are arrogant, greedy, and never satisfied. What do they devour? *People* (v. 5b). The cost of empires is always the multitudes of those enslaved or impoverished by them. The same is true today, whether one thinks in geopolitical terms or in terms of vast multinational commercial "empires."

So, yes, the Babylonians are evil—God knows that. But for this very reason, God now goes on to explain that he will not only *use* Babylon as the agent of his judgment on his own people (since Nebuchadnezzar would soon attack Jerusalem and carry off the people into exile), but later on he *will also judge Babylon itself*. That's what we now read in the remainder of chapter two, where the term "Woe" is repeated five times. Babylon, the agent of God's judgment, is also in the firing line as the target of God's judgment.

THE AGENT BECOMES THE TARGET

Habakkuk's message here is consistent with what his contemporary Jeremiah helped the people to understand in the midst of that tumultuous decade (597–587 BC) ending with the siege and destruction of Jerusalem by the Babylonian armies. Jeremiah had the same perspective as Habakkuk. God was using Babylon as the *agent* of his judgment, but God would also treat Babylon as the deserving *target* of his judgment.

We can see this understanding of events in the two documents that Jeremiah sent to the exiles in Babylon through the diplomatic postbag. The first was a letter to the exiles themselves (Jer 29); the second was a scroll of denunciation against Babylon (Jer 50–51). Looking at both of these will help us fill out and understand what Habakkuk also perceives.

Jeremiah's Letter to the Exiles

First, here's how the account of the letter begins:

> [1]This is the text of the letter that the prophet Jeremiah sent from Jerusalem to the surviving elders among the exiles and to the priests, the prophets and all the other people Nebuchadnezzar had carried into exile from Jerusalem to Babylon. [2](This was after King Jehoiachin and the queen mother, the court officials and the leaders of Judah and Jerusalem, the skilled workers and the artisans had gone

into exile from Jerusalem.) ³He entrusted the letter to Elasah son of Shaphan and to Gemariah son of Hilkiah, whom Zedekiah king of Judah sent to King Nebuchadnezzar in Babylon. It said:

⁴"This is what the LORD Almighty, the God of Israel, says to all those I carried into exile from Jerusalem to Babylon: . . ." (Jer 29:1–4)

Can you see the difference between the narrator's description of the event in verse 1 ("the people *Nebuchadnezzar* had carried into exile"), and God's description in verse 4 ("all those *I* carried into exile"; my italics in both cases)? Which was true? Well, both, of course.

Nebuchadnezzar and his soldiers did do the dirty work on the ground. But behind the hammer of Nebuchadnezzar was the hand of God. *God* had carried his people off into exile as an act of judgment, using Nebuchadnezzar as his tool. So, they needed to accept that what had happened to them was under God's sovereign control. They needed to settle down where they were and prepare for a long stay (two generations, at least).

Read the rest of the letter in Jeremiah 29:1–14 to find out what God wanted his people to do in the meantime (especially the surprising verse 7). But the main point was this: whatever *Babylon* had done was done under the command and control of *Yahweh the God of Israel*. And that is the first part of the lesson that God wanted Habakkuk also to understand before it happened, even if it was shockingly hard to grasp. Babylon was simply the agent of God's judgment.

Or, like the graphic image that Isaiah had used to portray the Assyrians a century earlier (Isa 10:5), the Babylonians, too, were simply a stick in the hand of God, a stick that God was using to flog his own people in judgment. That's a nasty image, to be sure, but it has one shred of consolation: the stick remains under the control and intentions of the one wielding it (Isa 10:15). God decides when enough is enough.

Jeremiah's Denunciation of Babylon

Secondly, here's how the great long scroll of denunciation begins (the scroll takes up the whole of Jeremiah 50–51):

> ¹This is the word the LORD spoke through Jeremiah the prophet concerning Babylon and the land of the Babylonians:
>
> > ²"Announce and proclaim among the nations,
> >> lift up a banner and proclaim it;
> >> keep nothing back, but say,
> > 'Babylon will be captured;
> >> Bel will be put to shame,
> >> Marduk filled with terror.
> > Her images will be put to shame
> >> and her idols filled with terror.'
> > ³A nation from the north will attack her
> >> and lay waste her land.
> > No one will live in it;
> >> both people and animals will flee away." (Jer 50:1–3)

You can read the rest of those two chapters, if you have the time and stomach for it. It is scorchingly clear that God saw the arrogance and violence and greed of Babylon, and would bring judgment on it. It would sink like a stone in the Euphrates. That's where the scroll of judgment was to be symbolically dropped (although Jeremiah or Baruch must have kept a copy)—for this is how the account ends:

> ⁵⁹This is the message Jeremiah the prophet gave to the staff officer Seraiah son of Neriah, the son of Mahseiah, when he went to Babylon with Zedekiah king of Judah in the

fourth year of his reign. [60]Jeremiah had written on a scroll about all the disasters that would come upon Babylon—all that had been recorded concerning Babylon. [61]He said to Seraiah, "When you get to Babylon, see that you read all these words aloud. [62]Then say, 'LORD, you have said you will destroy this place, so that neither people nor animals will live in it; it will be desolate forever.' [63]When you finish reading this scroll, tie a stone to it and throw it into the Euphrates. [64]Then say, 'So will Babylon sink to rise no more because of the disaster I will bring on her. And her people will fall.'" (Jer 51:59–64)

The point should be clear by now. The fact that God would use the Babylonians as his means of bringing judgment on Judah did not mean that God was blind to the wickedness of Babylon itself. Far from it—God will deal consistently with all guilty parties in his own time, including Babylon.

It seems that God wanted this explanation to be unmistakably clear—for the Israelites and for us who read the Old Testament Scriptures. Isaiah had the same message. Here's what we read in Isaiah, as he, too, announces God's judgment on Babylon:

> [5]Sit in silence, go into darkness,
>   queen city of the Babylonians;
> no more will you be called
>   queen of kingdoms.
> [6]I was angry with my people
>   and desecrated my inheritance;
> I gave them into your hand,
>   and you showed them no mercy.
> Even on the aged
>   you laid a very heavy yoke.
> [7]You said, "I am forever—
>   the eternal queen!"

> But you did not consider these things
>> or reflect on what might happen. (Isa 47:5–7)

God had used the Babylonians for punishment on Israel, but they had "exceeded their brief" in excessive violence and cruelty, and so they would be brought down for that evil.

The agent of God's judgment thus becomes the target of God's judgment.

Let's come back now to Habakkuk. God says that Babylon's evil ways will rebound on them. They will reap what they had sown. The tables will be turned. Those whom they had oppressed and exploited will rise up to taunt them:

> *Will not all of them taunt him with ridicule and scorn[?]* (2:6a)

And that prospect introduces the first of five Woes that fill the rest of the chapter. You can see the word there in verses 6, 9, 12, 15, and 19.

Now, this word *Woe* is not just a term of personal lament (e.g., "Woe is me!"). It is a pronouncement of judgment. It declares the outworking and consequences of God's curse on evil. God's moral order has been violated, and it will "bounce back" and "bite" those who are guilty of "crimes against humanity."

But before we explore those five Woes, let's think briefly about this reality that the Bible calls God's judgment.

THE CERTAINTY OF JUDGMENT

There is a certainty about God's judgment in at least two ways.

First, judgment is a *prophetic* certainty. God declares it and warns about it, so it is authorized and guaranteed by God's own character as the God who does not lie (v. 3). Judgment will come because God says so, and God's word can be trusted.

But, secondly, judgment is a *moral* certainty. God *must* deal with sin and evil if he truly is the righteous holy God of all creation. This is not suggesting that God is obliged to some moral standard outside himself. No—God himself *is* the ultimate standard of all truth, goodness, and justice. That is the essence of God being utterly holy. God cannot, therefore, simply coexist with evil eternally. So, in order for God to be faithful to his own character, God must ultimately deal with unrepentant evildoers also. There will be a reckoning, simply because Yahweh is the God he is. God is the sole and ultimate moral judge of the universe. As Abraham knew, the God of all the earth will do what is right (Gen 18:25).

Once we have grasped these truths about the certainty of God's judgment, we need to understand further that all this is *part of the gospel*. For it is indeed *good news* that evil will not have the last word. Evildoers will not, as we say, "get away with it" forever. Justice will be done by God in God's time. God will put all things right, while human justice can only ever be executed in partial, provisional, and incomplete (but still important and necessary) ways.

How should we respond to this part of the message of Habakkuk—and indeed of the whole Bible—about the judgment of God? I think the Bible gives us several proper reactions.

There is no doubt that the Bible talks about the ultimate destruction of the wicked as a matter of *horror and fear*. Habakkuk quaked and trembled in fear, as we'll see in chapter 3. We cannot contemplate this awful prospect without remembering that it is only by the grace of God in Christ that we can be spared it.

Judgment should also *grieve* us. The tears of Jeremiah as he foresaw the awful punishment bearing down on his people were just as much the tears of God himself (those tears blend together in Jeremiah 8:21–9:3, where it's hard to know whether the speaker is Jeremiah, God, or both). In Jeremiah 48 the grief and tears are certainly God's, and they are for the suffering of Moab under his judgment (Jer 48:31–32, 36). God takes no pleasure, insists Ezekiel, in the death of the wicked but rather that they would repent and live (Ezek 33:11). And when God inevitably has to act in punitive affliction, it is "not from his heart" says Lamentations 3:33 (the literal Hebrew translated as "not willingly" in the NIV). What brings grief to God's heart should surely bring grief to ours.

However, paradoxically, the certainty that God will come to judge the earth with his righteousness is ultimately a matter of *relief* and indeed of *joy* for all creation. Psalms 96 and 98 conclude with the resounding songs of all creation, rejoicing that there will be cosmic rectification—that is, to put all things right—when God comes to judge the earth. Evil and sin will not have the last word. In the book of Revelation, God's long-awaited throwing down of "Babylon" in chapter 18 (that is, when God has acted in final and irreversible judgment on the whole world of oppressive and destructive rebellion against God) brings forth four robust hallelujahs in chapter 19. God's just judgment on all wrongdoing is good news; it is part of the gospel.

Finally, we need to express unqualified *gratitude*, for we know that only through the cross of Christ have we ourselves been put right with God. For God in Christ bore the judgment that we deserve in God's own self, so that we can stand before him, now and on the last day, clothed in the righteousness of Christ.

With those perspectives in mind, let's now turn to the Woes that Habakkuk pronounces.

FIVE WOES

Habakkuk 2:6–20 gives us five portraits of the Babylonian Empire—and they are very unflattering portraits. "*Woe to* **him** . . ." (my emphasis) almost certainly, as I said earlier, means the king of Babylon as the representative embodiment of Babylon itself.

Now, as it turned out, the outworking of these Woes (that is, the exercise of God's judgment on Babylon), operated *within the history* of that era. The Babylonian Empire established by

Nebuchadnezzar lasted around seventy years before it, in turn, was defeated and replaced by the Persian Empire, which was vastly larger and lasted far longer. In fact, in world history terms, the Neo-Babylonian Empire was more like a short blip—a kind of exploding firework that awes and dazzles for a while and then disappears in darkness.

It would certainly not have felt like a blip if you were living in the midst of that empire as one of the exiles from Judah, like Daniel and his friends. But, even then, Daniel saw that Babylon was one of a sequence of human empires, all of which would ultimately fall before the rock of the reign of God and the authority of the one like a son of man. Empires come and empires go, but God's kingdom stands forever. That is how Daniel understood both Nebuchadnezzar's dream statue (Dan 2) and Daniel's own vision of beasts from the sea (Dan 7). Heaven rules, and God will work out his judgments within history. God's judgment, within the flow of history until the return of Christ, is a recurring event.

Thus, as we read Habakkuk 2, we are not reading about the "final judgment." Rather, this is one of those provisional and partial "rectifications" that God brings about within the ebb and flow of history. God puts down one king, nation, or empire and raises up another. Babylon is one such moment in the many threads of that great historical tapestry.

But, remember: God told Habakkuk that his message was to be recorded for others to hear (v. 2), and indeed this is a message with implications for "*all the earth*" (v. 20; see also v. 14). So, we are justified in extending what we read here beyond Babylon in the sixth century BC into all the centuries and empires ever since. We read what God saw in the sinful heart of the *Babylonian* Empire, and we can use this as a lens through which we can view what God sees in *today's world* also.

After all, the five things Habakkuk condemns here have certainly not gone away with the passing of Babylon. These are rather snapshots of some very characteristic evils of human powers, governments, empires, and tyrannies all through history—which reach their apocalyptic climax in the "Babylon" of Revelation. And we see these evils only too clearly at work in today's global empires—whether in political, economic, or cultural form.

1. Wealth by Plunder (2:6–8)

> [6]*"Woe to him who piles up stolen goods*
> *and makes himself wealthy by extortion!*
> *How long must this go on?"*
> [7]*Will not your creditors suddenly arise?*
> *Will they not wake up and make you tremble?*
> *Then you will become their prey.*
> [8]*Because you have plundered many nations,*
> *the peoples who are left will plunder you.*
> *For you have shed human blood;*
> *you have destroyed lands and cities and everyone*
> *in them. (2:6–8)*

Babylon, like all other conquering empires (including the British Empire), made itself very rich and luxurious, simply by stealing the wealth of other nations. Nebuchadnezzar so enriched Babylon that his famous Hanging Gardens became one of the Seven Wonders of the ancient world. And the habit continued.

In the fifteenth and sixteenth centuries, Spain and Portugal, which are now among the poorer nations of western Europe, became massively wealthy through trade and conquest, especially on the back of the silver and gold of South and Central America.

In the seventeenth and eighteenth centuries, the African slave trade simply stole vast quantities of human labour from Africa and used it mercilessly to increase the wealth of Britain, America, and Brazil, though Arab slave trading preceded the Atlantic trade and continued after its end.

In the eighteenth and nineteenth centuries, colonial expansion brought wealth from India, the Far East, and Africa into the industrializing European nations, particularly Britain, France, and Belgium.

Today, it's not so much imperial colonialism but multinational capitalism and astronomical individual greed that piles up wealth for some—often with no accountability. In the wake of the global financial crisis of 2008, some predatory banks continued to increase their wealth with scandalous treatment of struggling small businesses. The collapse of the Soviet Union and the Russian economy saw the emergence of so-called "oligarchs" who made a killing (sometimes literally) out of whole swathes of the former Russian economy, laundering their billions in London while the poor of that city (where I presently live) still struggle with insufficient, inadequate, or unsafe housing. Even the tragedy of the COVID-19 pandemic became the means for the richest men on the planet to see their wealth increase by billions day after day and then use it to compete as private space tourists rather than vaccinate the world.

Sometimes the tables are turned. And when this happens, then things can collapse very badly and very "suddenly" (v. 7).

The element of divine judgment in this is exposed in verse 8—beginning with the explanatory words "because" and "for." God's retribution will fall on those who have treated their fellow human beings so cruelly. And not just human beings suffer; even *the earth itself* has been oppressed by such plundering greed, as we are now finding out at terrible cost. Human deaths, creational damage, and urban blight—these compound calamities are captured better by the ESV here:

> *for the blood of man and violence to the earth,*
> *to cities and all who dwell in them. (2:8b ESV)*

This verse reminds me of the final devastating word of judgment in Revelation 11:18 (italics mine): "The time has come for judging the dead . . . and for destroying *those who destroy the earth.*"

2. Security Built on Oppression (2:9–11)

> *⁹Woe to him who builds his house by unjust gain,*
> *setting his nest on high*
> *to escape the clutches of ruin!*
> *¹⁰You have plotted the ruin of many peoples,*
> *shaming your own house and forfeiting your life.*
> *¹¹The stones of the wall will cry out,*
> *and the beams of the woodwork will echo it.*
> *(2:9–11)*

Nebuchadnezzar reigned for about forty-five years, and in that time he rebuilt and fortified Babylon immensely. He was extremely proud of it: "Is not this the great Babylon I have built as the royal residence, by my mighty power and for the glory of my majesty?" (Dan 4:30). That's what Nebuchadnezzar said to himself as he surveyed his city from the roof of his palace—"*his house . . . his nest on high*" (Hab 2:9).

A Greek historian, Herodotus, once described the city in detail.[1] Now we know Herodotus was given to some exaggeration, but even allowing for this, the impression is of a vast, heavily defended city. Try to imagine what Herodotus describes:

- A city with a 14-mile square wall, 300 feet high and 25 feet thick around the outside, with another wall 75 feet behind the first and a deep moat surrounding it
- 250 towers that were 450 feet high
- The river Euphrates flowing through the middle, with gates and bridges that closed at night
- Nebuchadnezzar's own palace and the Hanging Gardens, spectacular enough to be one of the Seven Wonders of the ancient world

---

1. Herodotus, *The Histories*, 1.178–184.

And all of this "*to escape the clutches of ruin!*" That is, this grand building project was all for Nebuchadnezzar's own privacy and security, as he sought to protect himself and his city from any danger of defeat or destruction. What he sought was fame and security (see Dan 4:30). What he would eventually get would be shame and loss. And if that fate did not come in Nebuchadnezzar's own lifetime, it certainly overtook one of his successors, Belshazzar, whom verse 10b could describe perfectly (see Dan 5).

Things are no different today. The super wealthy seek to build their security on their wealth, often gained by unjust or questionable means. They buy splendidly isolated and gated homes, and sometimes whole islands. They hire armed guards and all kinds of private security. And with their private jets and gigantic yachts, they avoid any collision with the ordinary public as they move around in their protected bubble.

The Panama Papers (in 2016), the Paradise Papers (in 2017), and the Pandora Papers (2021) have searingly exposed the lengths to which the super rich will go to hide their self-protecting wealth in secretive tax havens and shell companies. They avoid any accountability for how this wealth was obtained and shun any moral obligation to help the rest of the population by paying their taxes.

"You have plotted the ruin of many peoples." They did this back then, and they still do this today. Oxfam has estimated that developing countries lose an estimated $100–160 billion annually to corporate tax dodging, and this amount has probably increased vastly since the report was first published in 2013.[2]

However, as Habakkuk 2:11 puts it, the very stones and beams of the luxurious house built on oppression will cry out against the builder. This is a graphic way of saying that God is not fooled. God sees and hears and knows, and he will bring judgment on the

---

2. "Tax Evasion Damaging Poor Country Economies," Oxfam, September 1, 2013, https://www.oxfam.org/en/press-releases/tax-evasion-damaging-poor-country-economies.

oppressor, inevitably if not immediately. What was built on injustice will itself demand justice and bring ruin on those who perpetrated it, though sometimes this only happens generations later.

Proverbs 22:7–8 is a powerful commentary on these economic distortions. It both states a *fact* (that debt is a form of slavery, which is amply and tragically proven all over the world, including in our richest nations) and issues a *warning* (that injustice eventually bites back, causing terrible results in the long term):

> [7]The rich rule over the poor,
> and the borrower is slave to the lender.
>
> [8]Whoever sows injustice reaps calamity,
> and the rod they wield in fury will be broken.
> (Prov 22:7–8)

Historic injustice can last for centuries, poisoning all relationships and sowing seeds of pain and suffering that just go on and on and on. Sometimes later generations pay a heavy cost for the sins and oppression committed by their ancestors. We might think, for example, of:

- The legacy of genocide and slavery in the origins and early centuries of the USA, which goes on feeding racism and violence and societal divisions to this day
- The theft of land and dispossession of landowners in "the plantation of Ulster" in early seventeenth century Ireland, which sowed the seeds of religious and political strife and violence until the late twentieth century (these troubles have not yet been fully exorcised)
- The British Empire's colonial movements of whole populations for labour from one country to another, which underlie ongoing ethnic tensions in Sri Lanka and Myanmar (e.g., the Rohingya)

- The carving up of the former Ottoman Empire in the Middle East by Britain and France after the First World War (breaking promises made in several directions), effectively guaranteeing perpetual strife in the region for the following century

3. Transient Glory; God's Glory (2:12–14)

This passage continues the previous Woe, but expands it from Nebuchadnezzar's house to his city:

> *12Woe to him who builds a city with bloodshed*
> *and establishes a town by injustice!*
> *13Has not the LORD Almighty determined*
> *that the people's labor is only fuel for the fire,*
> *that the nations exhaust themselves for nothing?*
> *14For the earth will be filled with the knowledge of the glory*
> *of the LORD*
> *as the waters cover the sea. (2:12–14)*

This is the middle Woe of the five, and it is heavily laden with quotes and echoes of other scriptural texts, including its wonderful closing vision. These features probably mean that even though this Woe is like all the others, it anchors them all in solid hope—hope based on the knowledge that God is doing what his word says in other places (v. 12), that God is sovereign in the events he has "determined" (v. 13), and that the ultimate future of the earth is to be filled with the glory of Yahweh (v. 14).

Verse 12 echoes Micah 3:10. Micah (a century earlier) had condemned the rulers of Jerusalem "who build Zion with bloodshed, and Jerusalem with wickedness." Habakkuk extends Micah's declaration of God's judgment on Jerusalem to God's judgment on Babylon. Bloodshed and injustice, whether perpetrated by Israel or the nations, or by Christians or pagans, incur God's anger both in ancient times and today.

The city of Babylon had a great reputation. As I said, Nebuchadnezzar was very proud of it—so much so that he was eager to take personal credit (all governments are prone to take credit, whether deserved or not). He saw the city as a monument to his own quasi-divine presumptions of glory and majesty. Here is that boast again:

> Twelve months later, as the king was walking on the roof of the royal palace of Babylon, [30]he said, "Is not this the great Babylon I have built as the royal residence, by my mighty power and for the glory of my majesty?" (Dan 4:29–30)

"I have built . . ."??? Nebuchadnezzar probably never handled a brick in his life! Babylon was built, like all imperial cities, on the backs of the oppressed, the slaves, and the prisoners of war.[3] He built his own glory, and his own security, on the oppression of others and on "*bloodshed*" and "*injustice*" (v. 12). However, God's verdict on Nebuchadnezzar's city stands in stark contrast to his boast.

Human blood has a voice, as Cain discovered after the very first murder:

> [10]The Lord said, "What have you done? Listen! Your brother's blood cries out to me from the ground. [11]Now you are under a curse and driven from the ground, which opened its mouth to receive your brother's blood from your hand." (Gen 4:10–11)

This is also true with cities and whole civilizations that have been built on bloodshed. The poor and exploited masses who shed

---

3. In modern times, China is similarly alleged to be exporting prisoners to build roads and infrastructure in foreign lands. See Brahma Chellaney, "China's Newest Export: Convicts," *The Guardian*, July 29, 2010, https://www.theguardian.com/commentisfree/libertycentral/2010/jul/29/china-export-convict-labour.

their blood are now long forgotten—but not by God. Now, of course, we can also affirm that all human civilizations and great cities are evidence of human creativity and genius, the product of people made in the image of God and capable of great architecture, art, beauty, and culture. Cities are indeed astonishing evidence of human achievement. We can rightly enjoy and appreciate what they offer.

But there is a dark side that we ought not to forget when we visit big cities and admire their splendour:

- Tourists goggle at the buildings; God remembers the bloodshed.
- We are awed and impressed; God is not.
- We praise the great heroes immortalized in the names of streets and squares; God sees the suffering of those they exploited.
- We put up statues of the victors; God hears the cry of their victims.

Judgment follows inevitably in Habakkuk 2:13. Again, we hear other Scriptures. Verse 13 echoes Jeremiah 51:58, which comes in that scroll of God's judgment on Babylon which we referred to earlier:

> Babylon's thick wall will be leveled
>> and her high gates set on fire;
> the peoples exhaust themselves for nothing,
>> the nations' labor is only fuel for the flames. (Jer 51:58)

Habakkuk adds, however, "Has not the LORD Almighty determined . . . ?" (v. 13)

Now, the literal Hebrew reads, "Is it not, behold! from Yahweh of armies?" The rhetorical question is shaped to make a very strong affirmation: "Yes! It is indeed Yahweh, the one who controls the

hosts/armies of heaven and earth, who has determined this."
Babylon's armies will have enabled Nebuchadnezzar to enrich his
own city by violently crushing and despoiling other nations. But
the Babylonians will themselves end up in exhaustion and all of
Nebuchadnezzar's boasted labour will amount to nothing in the
end. This awesome war machine will eventually be consumed and
perish—for God says so.

This judgment will also fall upon all the empires of human
history. In the end, God blows them away into the sands of time.
All their effort and labour are, ultimately, in the grand scheme of
things, "for nothing." Where now are the great cities of the Incas,
the Mayas, the Babylonians, and even the Romans? Archaeological
ruins. And, yet, in their prime they must have felt indestructible,
unassailable, and everlasting.

Not so, says God—not then or now or ever.

This kind of national or imperial hubris is futile, exhausting,
and doomed to dust.

> Pride of man and earthly glory,
> Sword and crown betray his trust;
> What with care and toil he buildeth,
> Tower and temple fall to dust.
> But God's power, hour by hour,
> Is my temple and my tower.[4]

What a contrast then shines forth in Habakkuk 2:14! All the
transitory achievements of human pride, violence, and injustice
(vv. 12–13) will be replaced by the immeasurable and inextinguish-
able glory of God (v. 14). "Instead of being polluted with blood,
the earth will be permeated with glory."[5]

---

4. From the hymn "All My Hope on God Is Founded," by Joachim Neander and
translated by Robert Bridges.

5. David Prior, *The Message of Joel, Micah and Habakkuk*, The Bible Speaks Today
(Leicester, UK: IVP, 1998), 253.

Once again, Habakkuk is quoting and combining two Scriptures. The first is Numbers 14:21. There God speaks of his glory filling the whole earth, but at the same time tells the Israelites that the current generation would never set foot in the promised land because they had rebelled against him:

> [20]The Lord replied, "I have forgiven them, as you asked. [21]Nevertheless, as surely as I live and as surely as the glory of the Lord fills the whole earth, [22]not one of those who saw my glory and the signs I performed in Egypt and in the wilderness but who disobeyed me and tested me ten times—[23]not one of them will ever see the land I promised on oath to their ancestors." (Num 14:20–23)

However, the second Scripture is Isaiah 11:9, which comes as the climax to God's promise of the era of salvation, justice, and peace that will be ushered in by the future Davidic ruler. Environmental harmony will reign in creation:

> For the earth will be filled with the knowledge
> of the Lord
> as the waters cover the sea. (Isa 11:9b)

Habakkuk combines the "glory" of Numbers (a word of judgment) with the "knowledge" of Isaiah (a word of salvation), so that not only will God's glory fill the whole earth, but it will be seen and *known* to do so by the earth's whole population:

> *For the earth will be filled with the knowledge of the glory*
> *of the Lord*
> *as the waters cover the sea. (2:14)*

There is a sense in which God's glory *already* fills the whole earth—as Isaiah heard the seraphim calling out to one another

(Isa 6:3). Indeed, the fullness of the earth (its rich and plentiful biodiversity) is partly what constitutes the glory of God. But Habakkuk's point goes further: the earth will be filled with *the knowledge* of the glory of God.[6] This is Habakkuk's way of expressing the equally vast vision of Isaiah:

> And the glory of the LORD will be revealed,
>   *and all people will see it together.*
>   For the mouth of the LORD has spoken.
>   (Isa 40:5; my italics)

And notice also that it's *the earth* that will be filled with the knowledge of God's glory—not just heaven (which is filled already). We will not have to go off to heaven to know and see the glory of God. God's plan is to fill the *earth* with his glory, just as his glory came down at Mt. Sinai and filled the tabernacle and later the temple.

A great and glorious arch spans from Habakkuk 2:14 to the vision of John in Revelation 21. In that final scene, the glory of God and the proper glory of humanity—purged and cleansed of all sin, pride, deception, and violence (all the vainglory of Babylon)—will combine in the city of God:

> [23]The city does not need the sun or the moon to shine on it, for *the glory of God* gives it light, and the Lamb is its lamp. [24]The nations will walk by its light, and the kings of the earth will bring their splendor into it. [25]On no day will its gates ever be shut, for there will be no night there. [26]*The glory and honor of the nations* will be brought into it. [27]Nothing impure will ever enter it, nor will anyone who does what

---

6. In Arthur Campbell Ainger's great hymn, "God Is Working His Purpose Out as Year Succeeds to Year," only the demands of the metrical rhythm regrettably required him to omit Habakkuk's words "the knowledge of," so that the last line of each verse became, "when the earth shall be filled with the glory of God as the waters cover the sea."

is shameful or deceitful, but only those whose names are written in the Lamb's book of life. (Rev 21:23–27; my italics)

4. Degradation of Nations; Destruction of Nature (2:15–17)

> [15] *Woe to him who gives drink to his neighbors,*
>> *pouring it from the wineskin till they are drunk,*
>> *so that he can gaze on their naked bodies!*
> [16] *You will be filled with shame instead of glory.*
>> *Now it is your turn! Drink and let your nakedness*
>>> *be exposed!*
>> *The cup from the LORD's right hand is coming around*
>>> *to you,*
>> *and disgrace will cover your glory.*
> [17] *The violence you have done to Lebanon will*
>>> *overwhelm you,*
>> *and your destruction of animals will terrify you.*
> *For you have shed human blood;*
>> *you have destroyed lands and cities and everyone*
>>> *in them. (2:15–17)*

All empires humiliate, demean, and degrade those they conquer. The vanquished can be treated as less than human, slaughtered with the same impunity as rats or fleas. It's even boasted of as a service to the rest of humanity—here are some notorious examples:

- Rome crucified people—a practice so deliberately dehumanizing that it was not even to be thought or talked about in decent company.
- The British Empire committed some egregiously racist atrocities among "natives" in Africa and India. They also humiliated the Chinese through the opium trade (which the Chinese have not forgotten, even if most British people have).

- We all know of the Nazis' treatment of the Jews.
- The Burmese army's treatment of the Rohingya was allegedly justified by regarding them as "vermin."
- In modern genocidal conflicts, whole populations are systematically abused: such as the mass rape of women, intentionally shaming their menfolk who are powerless to save them, or the homosexual rape of men to humiliate them.
- We were revulsed by allegations of degrading treatment of prisoners in Iraq, Afghanistan, and elsewhere.
- The Russian invasion of Ukraine has been accompanied by multiple war crimes; rape, torture, and abuse of civilians; and the destruction of priceless cultural history.

All these examples—and many more—fit a pattern of glorifying one's own superiority by humiliating others or profiting from the exploitation of others—for example, through seduction and then trafficking:

> Whether that is the exploitation of cheap Chinese labourers, or Albanian and Russian women in European brothels, or the exploitation of children in sweatshops, or hostages in Iraq, or the trafficking of refugees—all of these are graphic illustrations of the appalling lack of regard for the dignity of others, the depraved behaviour of those who live their lives without God.[7]

Habakkuk's metaphor in verse 15 sounds like what we today would call "date rape," where a man gets a woman drunk or drugged and then abuses her sexually. But Habakkuk expands this metaphor to an international scale. The imperial power reduces

---

7. Jonathan Lamb, *From Why to Worship: A Journey through the Prophecy of Habakkuk* (Milton Keynes, UK: Authentic Media, 2007), 70.

the subject nation to abject impotence and then just takes what it wants for its own pleasure or enrichment. The smell of colonialism's toxic breath haunts such a description.

But, as God says in verse 16, ultimately the tables will be turned. That "cup" which arrogant empires have used to reduce others to drunken shame will become the cup of God's judgment. Another biblical arch, but not a glorious one, thus spans from Habakkuk 2:16 to the shaming and downfall of the great "prostitute" Babylon in Revelation 18. "She" is the one who had shamed others into allegiance and "trading" with her, and "she" will ultimately taste the punitive judgment of God ("a double portion from her own cup," Rev 18:6), on all her devouring oppressions.

The greed and violence of empires, ancient and modern, spreads even wider. Habakkuk 2:17 reminds us that empires not only kill and exploit human beings, but also perpetrate massive destruction on nature, on God's earth—a point that Habakkuk hinted at in verse 8.

"Lebanon" (v. 17a) stands not just for the country, but for the famous cedar forests of that land. Vast quantities of those magnificent trees were cut down in ancient times for various purposes—sometimes for machinery of war, sometimes for luxury homes (e.g., Solomon's palace, 1 Kgs 7, and Jehoiakim's palace, Jer 22:14–15). Assyria and Babylon also both devastated those cedars in their warmongering. The horrendous suffering of forests because of human warfare is noted by Isaiah in his prophecy of the fall of Babylon in chapter 14. He pictures not only the rejoicing of the *people* who would be liberated from oppression, but also the joy of lands and trees—which will no longer have to suffer when the king of Babylon lies dead:

> [7]All the lands are at rest and at peace;
>   they break into singing.
> [8]Even the junipers and the cedars of Lebanon
>   gloat over you and say,

"Now that *you* have been laid low,
    no one comes to cut *us* down." (Isa 14:7–8; my italics)

Also, along with the loss of trees went the "destruction of animals" through the obvious loss of habitat and excessive hunting (Hab 2:17). Unfortunately, not much has changed since then—except these predations are now perpetrated on a global scale.

And so Habakkuk 2:17b sums things up, repeating verse 8. Babylon was guilty of "the blood of man and violence to the earth" (ESV). These evils go together, then and now. People and land are often violated simultaneously. Some of the worst environmental destruction in today's world is accompanied by brutally suppressive practices against indigenous populations and murderous exploitation of workers. This is true for oil in southern Nigeria, mining and rubber in South America, jade in the Kachin province of Myanmar, cobalt in the Democratic Republic of the Congo, gold and diamonds in South Africa, palm oil or ranching in the Amazon rain forest, and the ecocidal destruction of arable land, crops, dams, and rivers in Ukraine. Environmental destruction is one of the most horrendous evils of our world during the past century and more.

Prudent guardianship of the earth is a part of biblical teaching that we often overlook. God the Creator cares about his "property," because "the earth is the LORD's, and everything in it" (Ps 24:1). He holds us responsible for how we treat the earth and condemns those who wantonly destroy it.

But in the end, says God in Habakkuk 2:17, what we have done to the natural world will "overwhelm" and "terrify" us. Is that not exactly what is happening in our generation? How frightening is the future for our planet, with the loss of so many species amounting to the sixth great mass extinction in the planet's biological history, the pollution and dying of the oceans and rivers, the depletion and loss of the soil on which our lives depend, and the breakdown of global climate patterns as a result of human-accelerated global warming? These things do indeed "terrify" those who think about them long enough. Lord, have mercy!

5. Idolatry, Confusion and Lies (2:18–19)

> [18]*Of what value is an idol carved by a craftsman?*
>   *Or an image that teaches lies?*
> *For the one who makes it trusts in his own creation;*
>   *he makes idols that cannot speak.*
> [19]*Woe to him who says to wood, "Come to life!"*
>   *Or to lifeless stone, "Wake up!"*
> *Can it give guidance?*
>   *It is covered with gold and silver;*
>   *there is no breath in it. (2:18–19)*

Once more, God comes back to the underlying sin of all—idolatry. That's where God's first description of Babylon ended: "[their] own strength is their god" (1:11). This is the idolatry of military superiority and national pride.

However, in this final "Woe!" God points to the way people give credence to the idols they have created for themselves. We put our faith in them, no matter how often they fail. We seem almost desperate to believe in them. This type of temptation may especially apply to those in power, since they "need" the gods to sustain their position. It's akin to "believing your own propaganda." First, you create a falsehood (i.e., "the big lie") and by ruthless repetition you demand that others believe it. Then when they do, you have to believe it yourself to make it "stick." The lie becomes a vicious, self-reinforcing feedback. It is astounding, sometimes, to listen to senior politicians, such as a president or a prime minister, and hear them boldly affirming something that they simply *must* know is a lie (since it may well have been already exposed as such by undeniable facts). In fact, they know that *we* know it is a lie, and yet they go on speaking with such passion and conviction as if their very status depended on us believing them. Idolatry of self and pride is lurking there, and the sacrifice demanded by those gods is the death of truth.

But this tendency does not afflict just elevated leaders, ancient or modern. It is also at the heart of idolatry for all of us. We *want* to believe in the gods we create, so we easily forget that they are nothing more than something we invented ourselves! The great thing about these idols, after all, is that you can make them support your own desires and choices. They *"cannot speak"*; *"there is no breath"* in them, as Habakkuk so trenchantly points out. So, these gods will never *challenge* what you are thinking or doing (unlike the living God). You made them for your own convenience, so they will support your ambitions (which may themselves be gods of a kind), bolstered by all sorts of plausible reinforcement from the surrounding culture. That's what gods are for. They give an air of sanctity and quasi-divine status to desires and demands of our own invention.

Yet, ironically, even though these idols can't speak, they *"teach lies"* (v. 18a)! Idols are dumb teachers, presiding over a whole curriculum of lies, deception, and falsehoods. It is easy to point a mocking finger at the more glaring examples, such as presidential claims that manifest falsehoods are simply "alternative facts," with any contradiction by factual reality being dismissed as "fake news." But at a more insidious level our cultures are permeated with lies—for example, about what does or does not benefit human life:

- There is the Mammon lie: greed is good; everything has its price; the market decides; the environment must be "economized."
- There is the Freedom lie: you are free to be whoever or whatever you want; nobody can or should exercise authority over your own free choices, especially in the sexual realm.
- There is the Self lie: you can be whatever you choose to be so long as you believe in yourself; self-fulfilment is the highest goal; you can create and decide your own identity (including your gender).

- There is the Security lie: as a state, or as an individual, you have to ensure your own safety, no matter what it costs in vastly expensive armaments or personal firearms—or the human blood they shed. False gods kill, none more ruthlessly than the gun god.

All lies, of course, however innocent their faces may look, bear the marks of Satan. As Jesus told us, Satan has been the "father of lies" from the very beginning (John 8:44). Yet people trust lies (Hab 2:18b)! We go on paying lip service to the very things that eventually let us down and destroy us. We refuse to stop believing these lies. We trust in our own creations—whether intellectual or technological.

In verses 18 and 19, Habakkuk exposes the stark contrast between the idols (all the false gods of his day and ours) and the one true living God of Israel, the God and Father of our Lord Jesus Christ and our God today:

- *They* are human constructs ("his own creation"); *the living God* is uncreated and eternal.
- *They* "teach lies"; *the living God* speaks truth and is the source of all truth.
- *They* claim our "trust"; *the living God* alone is to be the object of our faith (2:4).
- *They* are supposed to give us "guidance"; *the living God* has already given us his revealed law and wisdom and promises to guide those who seek him.

We have finally reached the end of this catalogue of arrogance and idolatry. God has pronounced, "*Woe!*" on each portrait of destructive human wickedness. Such behaviour, whether personal or international, will inevitably end in tears—tears of self-inflicted loss and ruin. God's curse and God's judgment will work themselves out in the inevitable processes of human sin *rebounding on its perpetrators*. Evil done generates evil suffered.

After all, in each of the five portraits the *seeds of judgment lie within the sin itself.* This truth is built into God's moral universe. You reap what you sow. Sin has evil consequences, and those evil results boomerang back on the head of the sinner, individual or corporate. Can you see it in each case which follows?

- The plundered become the plunderers (v. 8).
- The stones and wood of the luxury palace built on the ruin of other humans cry out against the builder (v. 11).
- The toil of nations will exhaust the nations with their own futility (v. 13).
- The cup used to humiliate others will come around to pour judgment down the throat of the perpetrator and the cruelty done to nature will terrify the violent (vv. 16–17).
- The idol that is trusted is actually unable to even wake up, let alone save or guide its worshipers (v. 18).

SILENCE!

But we must give God the last word, for indeed he has the last word in this turbulent chapter. It comes, in verse 20, in stark contrast to all the wretched kaleidoscope of evil and judgment in the five Woes:

> The LORD is in his holy temple;
>   let all the earth be silent before him. (2:20)

God announces the cosmic truth that stands above and beyond all human idolatries—*The LORD God himself is in charge,* and we need to shut up and pay attention.

Now, when the verse says that "*The LORD is in his holy temple,*" it does not mean that God is hiding in a building—whether the temple in Jerusalem or any church building today. That's where many politicians would like to keep him! When the church speaks out against political evil, we are told to go back to our pulpits and stick to "spiritual matters." The assumption is that God has no place in the public arena. Western culture has been saying this for three hundred years, ever since the Enlightenment and the emergence of secular materialism and humanistic European culture. The philosophical dualism that separated the public and private spheres (that is, it separated the world of so-called objective science, empirical facts, and reason from the world of subjective religion, dogmas, and faith) confined God to the latter sphere and firmly prohibited him from wandering unchallenged around the other one.

God has been banished from the public square.

But no, says Habakkuk. "*The LORD is in his holy temple,*" which means in *the seat of government.* God's temple means the dwelling place of God. Furthermore, the temple, in ancient Near Eastern and biblical thought, is the place from which God (or the gods) exercised their rule. It was the CEO's office. To say that God is in his temple means that God is actively sovereign over all that his temple governs. And the living God claims nothing less than the whole creation as his temple: "Heaven is my throne, and the earth is my footstool" (Isa 66:1). God rules in heaven *and on earth.*

Therefore, our proper posture is to kneel before God in quiet submission. "Let all the earth be silent before him."

Including Habakkuk!

Yes, God allowed Habakkuk's questions, and God still allows ours too. But in the end God calls us to settle down in quiet faith and trusting submission to his sovereign governance of the world. Now, as we shall see in the next chapter, Habakkuk will not exactly stay silent. On the contrary, he will burst into song with musical accompaniment! But his song will express and expand the truth of this final verse of chapter 2 and bring it to a resounding climax.

So then, in conclusion, let's remember the *three bright lights* that shine through the terrible gloom of this chapter's five Woes.

In verse 4, God calls the righteous to live by faith. We will be counted among the righteous only as we put our faith in the living God and receive God's gift of life. And, having started our journey of life by saving faith, *we are then to go on living by faith*, trusting and obeying the God who has given us life and put us right with himself. We will be faithful to him, and we will trust him even in the midst of a world we don't understand. Faithfulness does not mean having all the right answers. It means living in the right relationship. It means trusting that God will ultimately put things right and then leaving the questions, even the unanswered ones, in God's trustworthy hands.

In verse 14, God gives the righteous hope for the glory-filled future. God's ultimate mission is—and always has been—to restore the earth to its original purpose: to be filled with God's own glory, for our joy and blessing. This hope must have been part of what Paul had in mind when he articulated the mission of God in these words that come in the middle of a single Greek sentence (Eph 1:3–14), in which the word "glory" appears three times:

> [9][God has] made known to us the mystery of his will according to his good pleasure, which he purposed in Christ, [10]to be put into effect when the times reach their fulfilment—to bring unity to all things in heaven and on earth under Christ. (Eph 1:9–10)

Paul's mind was certainly filled when he contemplated the glory-filled future for the whole creation that will accompany our ultimate redemption:

> [18]I consider that our present sufferings are not worth comparing with the *glory* that will be revealed in us. [19]For the creation waits in eager expectation for the children of God to be revealed. [20]For the creation was subjected to frustration, not by its own choice, but by the will of the one who subjected it, in hope [21]that the creation itself will be liberated from its bondage to decay and brought into the freedom and *glory* of the children of God. (Rom 8:18–21; my italics)

In the midst of all our wrestling and questioning in a world we don't understand, we look forward to a world we can scarcely imagine.

In verse 20, God calls us to accept his sovereignty. This, of course, is the firm ground for the faith of verse 4 and the hope of verse 14. In a world awash with the idols of every culture—including our own—we look to the holy temple of the living God, where God exercises his cosmic government of both time and space and nature and history. Our sovereign God understands the world in ways we cannot. God knows the world he created, the world we have corrupted, the world he loved so much that he sent his only Son, the world he has reconciled to himself through the blood of the cross, and the world he will renew, restore, and fill with his glory.

As we rest in such revelation from God himself, we can be silent before him, content to live with faith and hope when understanding fails.

QUESTIONS FOR REFLECTION OR DISCUSSION

1. Do you agree that God's ultimate judgment is part of the gospel? And even if we can believe this judgment to be good news, how do you respond, emotionally and spiritually, to the Bible's insistence that God will judge the world?

2. Do any of the "five Woes" in Habakkuk 2 address specific issues in today's world, in your perception? Do you agree that idolatry is a fundamental root of all of these issues, as Paul suggests in Romans 1?

3. If God's "holy temple" (v. 20) is the seat of his sovereign government, what does it mean in practice to "be silent before him" (if, presumably, it does not just mean that we don't say another word!)?

CHAPTER 5

TRUSTING GOD'S WORD

Habakkuk 3:1–19

Before we embark on Habakkuk's final chapter, let's remind ourselves how this journey has gone so far. We've listened in on Habakkuk's conversation with God as he wrestled with circumstances in his own country that angered him, as well as forthcoming events in the wider world that alarmed him. Twice Habakkuk has raised his questioning protest, and twice God has answered. It has been a tough conversation! It seems that Habakkuk is struggling with both the world he cannot understand and the God he cannot understand.

We know how he feels.

However, out of the dialogue thus far I think we can clearly see two significant points.

First—the absolute certainty of the destruction of evil and the triumph of God. God will not tolerate evil forever. While his ways may seem strange right now, God not only works to bring down oppressors within the long arc of history, but he will also ultimately bring an end to all oppression and suffering for humanity and nature. God's justice is operating within history (even if only partially at present), and it will be fully and irrevocably exercised at the end of history when "the Judge of all the earth" (Gen. 18:25) will do what is right, beyond question or complaint.

This is an encouraging truth, and it means that we should not *envy* the ungodly when they seem so rich and powerful. We should rather pity them and, indeed, pray for them. For unless they come to repentance, their end is terrible indeed. This was the insight that the psalmist Asaph realized when he turned from his frustration with the prosperity of the wicked and went into God's presence:

> [16]When I tried to understand all this,
>   it troubled me deeply
> [17]till I entered the sanctuary of God;
>   then I understood their final destiny.
>
> [18]Surely you place them on slippery ground;
>   you cast them down to ruin.
> [19]How suddenly are they destroyed,
>   completely swept away by terrors!
> [20]They are like a dream when one awakes;
>   when you arise, Lord,
>   you will despise them as fantasies.
>   (Ps 73:16–20)

Second—that there are two ways to live, and we have to choose (2:4). One choice is the way of unbelief, arrogance, and crookedness—the way that will eventually engulf us under the woes of God's wrath and judgment. The other is the way of faith and faithfulness. The one who walks in this second way knows, trusts, and obeys God, thereby living among the righteous (as pictured in Psalm 1). This does not remove or even reduce the challenges, evils, and tumult of the world around us. These trials are utterly real, frightening, and baffling. But we face them with faith in the wisdom, sovereignty, and ultimate purposes of God. We are called to live by faith, and then, being righteous by faith, we shall truly live. Such a way of living is a clear choice, a decision, and a commitment.

This living by faith happens daily. It does indeed begin with that first act of putting our faith in Christ and being made right with God, in the classic sense of justification by grace through faith alone—a faith that demonstrates itself in obedience. And this beginning guarantees the ending—that is, that those who are thus justified by God are assured of being among the righteous in glory on the last day. That is the comforting sequence of affirmations in Romans 8:29–30. But from that first act of faith until its ultimate consummation in glory, we live every day in renewed trust in the sovereign good governance of God in God's world. We choose to do so. We are determined to do so. We insist on doing so, even in the midst of all that opposes, questions, or denies the goodness and sovereignty of God.

So, in response to all this, what does Habakkuk do? Well, he makes that choice, decision, and commitment. He turns from protest to prayer (3:1).[1] Or, rather, to song; for his prayer is indeed a song, for which he even provides the tune and the instruments (vv. 1 and 19)!

It is a mark of believers in all ages that they *sing*! Even in the midst of struggles and suffering, they sing. So many of the psalms are sung out of the depths of loneliness, illness, false accusation, or violent opposition. But they still sing. Paul and Silas, chained up in the bloody agony and post-traumatic stress of a Roman flogging, sing hymns in jail (Acts 16:22–25)! Jesus and his disciples sing the psalms of the Great Hallel (Pss. 134, 135, and 136) towards the end of their last meal together before his blood was shed (Matt 26:30). Christians all over the world today sing, even those living in desperate poverty and suffering. Even up to the point of martyrdom, their voices keep singing!

So, let's try to sing along with Habakkuk as he recalls God's character, God's story, and God's word.

---

1. Habakkuk seems to generate these alliterative transitions, as Jonathan Lamb puts it in the title of his exposition of Habakkuk, *From Why to Worship*. Martyn Lloyd-Jones does similarly in his *From Fear to Faith*.

HABAKKUK REQUESTS FRESH PROOF OF GOD'S CHARACTER (3:1–2)

> ¹*A prayer of Habakkuk the prophet. On shigionoth.*
>
> ²LORD, *I have heard of your fame;*
> *I stand in awe of your deeds,* LORD.
> *Repeat them in our day,*
> *in our time make them known;*
> *in wrath remember mercy. (3:1–2)*

Habakkuk begins by acknowledging what he has heard already. Like any Israelite, he knows (from the psalms and stories of his people) what God has done in the past, and God has just told him what he is doing in the present and what God plans to do in the future.

The words "*your deeds*" in verse 2 is actually singular in Hebrew: "your work." It may be a deliberate echo of 1:5, where God had said that he is "working a work." Well, Habakkuk sure knows now what that "work" of God is. That is, he knows God's reputation ("your fame") for amazing past deeds (which he will sing about in a moment), *and also* he knows from God's word to him what God plans to do in the future (in relation to Babylon and all evil empires).

Knowing these things, Habakkuk says, "*I stand in awe.*" Indeed, his words are stronger than that. "I'm scared!" he says. "*Your work, O* LORD, *do I fear*" (ESV). It is indeed comforting, of course, to know that God is sovereign and is governing all human history. But it can still be pretty terrifying when you perceive what is coming down the pipe! It is certainly reassuring to know that God is the one who has raised up the Babylonians, and that God will ultimately judge them, too, for their evil ways. But that doesn't make it any easier to contemplate in advance what they will do to Jerusalem and God's people.

So, Habakkuk has two requests.

1. That God Would Be at Work Today as He Had Been in the Past

The phrases "*in our day*" and "*in our time*" are exactly the same expression in Hebrew: "in the midst of the years," which is repeated for emphasis. What Habakkuk seems to mean is: "Lord, in between your past actions in history and your future judgment yet to come, be at work right here and now in such a way that people will come to know who you are. Make yourself known *now!*"

This is a prayer for God to show his power, for the sake of his own name and reputation.[2] It's a prayer that we find in many of the psalms, and we still pray it. It goes something like this:

> *Lord, we know what you did in the past (we've read our Bibles!), and we know what you're going to do in the ultimate future (the Bible tells us that too). But, in the meantime, here we are now, longing for you to act in this corrupt and evil world which we struggle to understand. Please make yourself known by showing us signs of your justice and salvation at work. Humble the proud. Defeat the oppressor. Rescue the downtrodden. Save the lost. Do your work, Lord! Be the God we know you are!*

Even in our current society, which refuses to acknowledge God, we ought to be praying for God to be at work. We must ask him to bring down the proud and wicked and defend and care for the poor and needy. We must pray *for* our government and leaders (Paul tells us to do this), but sometimes we also have to pray *against* them when they are doing injustice (the psalmists show

---

2. Habakkuk 3:1 in the KJV ("*O LORD, revive thy work in the midst of the years*") became the inspiration for a hymn that Christians of a certain age may remember:

> Revive thy work, O LORD,
> Thy mighty arm make bare;
> Speak with the voice that wakes the dead,
> And make thy people hear. (Albert Midlane, 1858)

us how to do this). There is no contradiction in doing both, for there is no contradiction in the "work" of God, which embraces both God's mercy *for* sinners (who, we pray, will repent and turn to Christ for salvation) and God's anger *against* those who wilfully perpetrate injustice, lies, and violence. This leads to the other part of Habakkuk's prayer.

2. That When God Acts in Wrath, He Would Remember Mercy

"*In wrath remember mercy.*" Such a powerful prayer! And it is all the more emphatic for being just three short words in Hebrew. The literal rendition of these words is, in this order:

- "In raging anger
- to show compassion
- remember."

The contrast (from our point of view) between anger and compassion, and between wrath and mercy, is made all the more stark by putting the words side by side and then pleading with God to "remember" the second word—as if God could ever "forget" the compassion that defines his very nature.

This profound prayer is so true and central to what Habakkuk knew about God (as we do too) from the whole revelatory story of Scripture. Habakkuk knows two things with certainty.

First, *Habakkuk knows God's righteous anger* (both against Israel and against Babylon and other nations). He was a prophet, after all—one of that long line of men and women, through generations of Israel's history from Moses onwards, who shuddered and thundered at the force of God's implacable opposition to all that offends and frustrates his love and his good purposes for human and creational flourishing. If God were *not* angry against sin and evil, injustice and brutality, greed and poverty, and lust and abuse, what kind of God would he be? The idea that "God's wrath" is just a medieval myth that we should abandon today is simply incompatible not only with the whole Bible (including the teaching of Jesus), but also with our own instincts and moral outrage when we see evil done with impunity. If *we* rage in anger when evildoers "get away with it" laughingly scot-free, within the limited frame of our own awareness, what might we imagine is *God's* reaction, in the infinite frame of God's awareness of all the wickedness of all humanity in all the earth in all history? "Raging anger" is not too strong a phrase, is it?

But *Habakkuk also knows God's compassion and mercy.* This is Yahweh's defining character. Indeed, it is the self-identifying name badge that God revealed to Moses from the very start of Israel's journey with God at Mt. Sinai:

> 5Then the LORD came down in the cloud and stood there with him and proclaimed his name, the LORD. 6And he passed in front of Moses, proclaiming, "The LORD the LORD, the compassionate and gracious God, slow to anger, abounding in love and faithfulness, 7maintaining love to thousands, and forgiving wickedness, rebellion and sin. Yet he does not leave the guilty unpunished; he punishes the children and their children for the sin of the parents to the third and fourth generation." (Exod 34:5–7)

Now, we can immediately see a tension in those famous words (quoted frequently throughout the rest of the Old Testament), between the wonderful words of verses 6–7a and the final sentence at the end—"Yet . . ." But in this context, both parts of God's speech perfectly reflect the events that had just preceded them in the ghastly story of Exodus 32–33—a story Habakkuk knew well. The Israelites had committed a terrible sin, involving idolatry with a golden bullock. God had indeed acted to punish the guilty, and yet had also chosen to forgive (literally, to "carry") the people in response to Moses's intercession.

There is mystery and paradox here, as we see both dimensions of God's character in action in the same events:

> So, Yahweh is the God who punishes *and* the God who forgives. Yahweh is the God of wrath *and* the God of grace and compassion. We cannot allow the second part of each sentence to eliminate the first. But our text will also not allow us to set these things in a simple equation, as if love and wrath are equivalent and opposite motions or emotions within God. Rather, we have *five* declarations of grace in one form or another and *one* of judgment. And we have the explicit contrast of love to *thousands* with punishment to "*third and fourth*."[3]

> The point is not that the people experience *either* wrath *or* mercy, but that both wrath and mercy are in the character of God though it is his mercy which is ultimately predominant in his dealings with his people.[4]

This is the character of the God Habakkuk knows, worships, and trusts. He accepts the reality and necessity of God's anger against evil, *and* he prays for God to exercise his mercy and grace, even in the midst of wrath.

This is a double truth about God that we find hard to grasp simultaneously in our finite minds. Nevertheless, we must hold on firmly to both parts.

In the end, this tension is only ultimately resolved on the cross of Christ, where wrath and mercy met. On the cross, God's wrath and God's mercy combined: his wrath borne and suffered by and within God himself, and his mercy outpoured by God in self-giving saving love:[5]

---

3. Christopher J. H. Wright, *Exodus: The Story of God Bible Commentary* (Grand Rapids: Zondervan Academic, 2021), 584 (italics original).

4. R. W. L. Moberly, *At the Mountain of God: Story and Theology in Exodus 32–34* (Sheffield, UK: JSOT Press, 1983), 87; my italics.

5. For this reason, I would love a simple change in one line of Keith Getty and Stuart

For at the cross, both truths about the character and action of God were acted out simultaneously and to the utmost. God finally did not, indeed, leave the guilty unpunished, but in order to "justify the ungodly," God the Holy Trinity chose to bear the consequences of sin and guilt in God's own self, in the person of the Son of God, who knew no sin but was made to "be sin" for us. In that great cosmic act, in which the Judge became the judged in our place, God demonstrated all that he had declared about himself as Yahweh, God of Israel, the compassionate and gracious God, carrying sin and abounding in love.[6]

So Habakkuk prays earnestly, "LORD, *in wrath remember mercy*."

And God whispers back, "I will, Habakkuk, I will. And you have no idea what it will cost me to do so."

HABAKKUK REMEMBERS THE STORY OF GOD'S POWER (3:3–15)

We move on into the central section of Habakkuk's prayer-song. And immediately we find ourselves in a wild poetic picture gallery of scenes from Israel's past history. We should not imagine any of the lines in a literalistic way. This is poetry, and the imagery is a combination of metaphors mixed in with historical allusions, some of which are obvious and some rather ambiguous. Habakkuk is remembering real history on this earth: things that really happened and things that God really did. But he is using the imaginative language of poetry and metaphor to describe their significance.

The tumbling torrent of images portrays the overwhelming

Townend's magnificent hymn "In Christ Alone." Instead of us singing that God's wrath (only) was satisfied, I would prefer us celebrating that *both* God's wrath and love were satisfied.

6. Wright, *Exodus*, 585.

experience of God *coming*. Throughout the Old Testament, in different ways and occasions, God's arrival was dramatic, spectacular, and sometimes literally earthshaking. Habakkuk's language here is drawn from the conceptual world of the great cosmic battle in which Yahweh, the God of Israel, is at war with all the forces of evil and wins his glorious victory over them. Such language is also found in the Psalms and persists into some of the visions of John in Revelation.

A key feature of all this poetry, in view of the point we've just been exploring, is that the actual historical events combined both the *wrath* of God against the wicked and the *mercy* of God bringing salvation and deliverance to his people. These are the highlights of God's story, which reassured Habakkuk that his prayer, "in wrath remember mercy," was not out of order but very much in line with God's own track record.

3:3–4

> ³God came from Teman,
>   the Holy One from Mount Paran.
> His glory covered the heavens
>   and his praise filled the earth.
> ⁴His splendor was like the sunrise;
>   rays flashed from his hand,
>   where his power was hidden.

These verses refer to the events at Mt. Sinai, specifically as recorded in Exodus 19. Teman and Paran were poetic names for the deep south, the region of Sinai (Num 10:12; Deut 33:1–2). Psalm 68:7–10 and Judges 5:4–5 picture Sinai as the place from which Yahweh "marched" forward with his people to the promised land.

3:5

> Plague went before him;
>   pestilence followed his steps.

This most likely alludes to the plagues (literally, "blows") that struck Egypt before the great exodus deliverance of Israel.

3:6–7

> ^{6}He stood, and shook the earth;
>> he looked, and made the nations tremble.
>
> The ancient mountains crumbled
>> and the age-old hills collapsed—
>> but he marches on forever.
>
> ^{7}I saw the tents of Cushan in distress,
>> the dwellings of Midian in anguish.

The God of all creation can make even mountains tremble and melt (this imagery for international turbulence surfaces again in Psalm 46:2–3). As Yahweh marches into Canaan at the head of the Israelites, the nations also tremble in fear—as Moses in an earlier song had said they would (Exod 15:14–16) and as Rahab later confirmed that they did (Josh 2:8–13).

3:8–10a

> ^{8}Were you angry with the rivers, LORD?
>> Was your wrath against the streams?
>
> Did you rage against the sea
>> when you rode your horses
>> and your chariots to victory?
>
> ^{9}You uncovered your bow,
>> you called for many arrows.
>
> You split the earth with rivers;
>> ^{10a}the mountains saw you and writhed.

Habakkuk's song now turns to address God himself again: "*You . . . LORD.*" These are rhetorical questions expecting the answer, "No, of course not." God was not angry with the actual sea and rivers and mountains. Rather, God used these natural features of his own creation to mediate his anger against his enemies. The pictorial language seems to have in mind the crossing of the Sea of Reeds, and later of the River Jordan, although "split[ting] the earth with rivers" may allude to the provision of water from the rock in the wilderness (Exod 17:1–7).

3:10b

Torrents of water swept by;
    the deep roared
    and lifted its waves on high.

This could be an allusion to the victory of Deborah over Sisera and the Canaanites, which was accomplished partly, it seems, because the River Kishon flooded, immobilizing their chariots (Judg 4:7, 13; 5:21).

3:11

Sun and moon stood still in the heavens
    at the glint of your flying arrows,
    at the lightning of your flashing spear.

The reference is most probably to Joshua's victory over the Amorites in Joshua chapter 10.

3:12–15

[12] In wrath you strode through the earth
    and in anger you threshed the nations.
[13] You came out to deliver your people,
    to save your anointed one.
You crushed the leader of the land of wickedness,
    you stripped him from head to foot.
[14] With his own spear you pierced his head
    when his warriors stormed out to scatter us,
gloating as though about to devour

> *the wretched who were in hiding.*
> *¹⁵You trampled the sea with your horses,*
> *churning the great waters.*

These verses could describe many occasions when God delivered his people from their enemies, but the mention of the sea again in verse 15 makes it likely that Habakkuk has returned to the great deliverance *par excellence*—the exodus, which acted as the model for all of God's redemptive acts until the death and resurrection of Christ.

What Habakkuk is doing in this poetic recital of the mighty acts of God is similar to what David does when he celebrates how God delivered him from the hand of Saul. Take a look at Psalm 18:6–17, in which David describes a "simple" historical rescue: God had prevented Saul from killing him. But he adorns this deliverance with vast cosmic, creational imagery very similar to Habakkuk's. In his desperate need, David felt like God had moved heaven and earth just to rescue him from certain death.

In fact, Habakkuk's song is a blend of language and themes from the song of *Moses* (Exod 15), the song of *Deborah* (Judg 5), and the song of *David* (Ps 18). Habakkuk knew his hymnbook! It would be worth pausing here to read quickly through those three great historic songs from centuries earlier. Take note of the similarities in language, imagery, and atmosphere to the song of Habakkuk. Can you see now how Habakkuk is using the great scriptural stories of the mighty acts of God to strengthen his own faith?

This seems to have been a good way during Old Testament times in Israel to boost one's faith and confidence in God's power to save. We can still do this today.

Sing the songs! Remember the stories!

Habakkuk, then, in this central part of his prayer-song, is drawing on the rich heritage of Israel's history, Israel's Scriptures, and Israel's songs. And he is doing this *in order to reinforce his own personal faith*. He is reliving the work of God in his own imagination. He is putting himself into the story, imagining every-thing again almost as an eyewitness.

This is the story he is in.

This is the people to whom he belongs.

This is the God in whom he trusts.

Ultimately, the effect of composing and singing this cele-bration of God's story with God's people is twofold:

First, it confirms God's word in chapters 1–2.

God had insisted on his power to act in judgment against the wicked, the violent, and the oppressor—including those within his own people. God had also declared his "Woes" upon the godless arrogant empire, even though he had used it as the agent of his judgment on Israel. This lesson was threaded through Israel's history. God will be victorious over all evil forces that oppose his mission, and God had proved this in Israel's past again and again. God, not the forces or doers of evil, will always have the last word. God can be trusted to do justice in the end.

Secondly, it confirms Habakkuk's faith that "we will not die" (1:12).

God's action in history had always been to defend his people from ultimate destruction, even in those times when God used foreign enemies as the agent of his judgment upon them. Of course, many *individual* people would be slain in the horrors of such judgment. Death on a massive scale would certainly happen when Babylon invaded Judah. Check out the book of Lamentations . . .

But *God's people as a whole* will be preserved. "*We* will not die." We the people, we the people of God, *we* will not be completely wiped out. Why not? Ultimately, we will be delivered because of God's promise to Abraham that through him and his people all nations on earth will be blessed.

Habakkuk does not mention the Abrahamic promise here, but it is undoubtedly the backstory underlying everything else. The God of Sinai introduced himself to Moses as the God of Abraham, Isaac, and Jacob (Exod 3:6), the God to whom all nations and the whole earth belong (Exod 19:5). This is God's mission, God's great long-term plan, and God's agenda for all history, all nations, and all creation. Because God will be faithful to that universal purpose, he will never allow his enemies (human or satanic) to triumph or his people to be destroyed.

Habakkuk, then, finds his reassurance ("we shall not die") by rehearsing the Bible story, the story of God, the story of promises made and promises fulfilled, the story of mighty acts of redemption, and the story of a people who will not die.

And so should we.

After all, we know a lot more of the story than Habakkuk did. We know its central climax at Calvary and the empty tomb, and we know its glorious conclusion in the city of God, the new creation.

We may not understand the *world* we are in, but we do know the *story* we are in. And we need to strengthen our faith by continually bringing this story to mind. In fact, this is the essential key to understanding the otherwise impossible way that Habakkuk now finishes his prayer-song.

HABAKKUK RESOLVES TO LIVE BY FAITH IN GOD'S WORD (3:16–19)

We now come to the end of Habakkuk's song and the end of his book. How do we find our prophet now? Happy-clappy, all smiles, and cheerful? Do we find Habakkuk singing "Three Little Birds" with Bob Marley, reassuring us that everything will just be all right? Not at all. We find him still shaking with fear, because God has shown him what lies ahead in the immediate future.

However, we also find Habakkuk strengthened in faith. He is determined to be among the righteous who will put their trust in God and go on living by faith (2:4)—no matter what. So, in these closing words Habakkuk makes three amazingly strong resolutions: I will wait. . . . I will rejoice. . . . I will run.

Resolved to Wait—in the Face of Paralyzing Fear (3:16)

> *I heard and my heart pounded,*
> > *my lips quivered at the sound;*
> *decay crept into my bones,*
> > *and my legs trembled.*
> *Yet I will wait patiently for the day of calamity*
> > *to come on the nation invading us. (3:16)*

This verse is brutally honest. Habakkuk tells us that his heart, his lips, his bones, and his legs are all quivering with fear. This man is an emotional wreck. He has lost control of his speech and his limbs. He is on the verge of mental and physical collapse. Why?

God's word has struck deep into Habakkuk's soul, and he "sees" what lies ahead for his own people. Invasion by Babylon will bring suffering and death and national humiliation such as Israel had never experienced before. The horror of it all breaks Habakkuk's heart and fills him with dread. The same emotions also overwhelmed Jeremiah, who was having the same prophetic premonitions of the catastrophe that was coming. In response, he simply wept and wept until he wished his whole head were made of water (Jer 9:1).

But this is the painful irony: *this agonizing awareness is the result of what Habakkuk had prayed for!* Remember, right at the start of his book Habakkuk had asked God to *do* something about the evil and wickedness going on in his own country (1:2–4). Then God had said, "I will. In fact, my response is already on the way. I am going to bring terrible judgment on Judah, and here's how: Babylon will invade and conquer it."

Habakkuk knows with searing clarity the unspeakable suffering and death that would follow in the ghastly and cruel warfare of that ancient world: military invasion, humiliating defeat in battle, obliteration of farms and homes, prolonged agony of urban siege, starvation and disease, breach of the city walls, slaughter, rape and rampage, capture, torture, and exile. Just glance through the book of Lamentations and you'll know the horror of what Habakkuk was anticipating. The familiar world he knew was collapsing around him in his imagination and would very soon crumble in reality. No wonder Habakkuk shuddered in fear.

Is our present situation any different?

For some people in our world, what I have just described is already part of the reality of life (and death) in war-torn, famine-ridden countries like Syria, Yemen, Ethiopia, the Democratic Republic of the Congo, Ukraine, and others. But the signs of a greater global collapse are also frightening. Climate chaos is already devastating some of the poorest countries in our world, and is impacting the poorest people even in the richest countries. Droughts, floods, fires, heat waves and big freezes, and extreme weather phenomena such as grossly intensified hurricanes and rainfall pay no respect to riches or poverty. It is hard to be optimistic about humanity's ability to slow down the processes that are causing the inexorable rise of the global temperature and its effects. The future seems dire, even in the best-case scenarios.

On top of this, the COVID-19 pandemic has not completely gone away, and there are fears it may rebound in new mutations. It is almost beyond belief how something so infinitesimally small as a virus could combine with human folly, political corruption, and arrogant complacency to cause such lethal and economic devastation on a global scale. Yet even this has happened before, as the "Spanish Flu" pandemic just over one hundred years ago showed, not to mention earlier horrific plagues.

And what of Western civilization as a whole? After five hundred years of its increasing global domination through the eras of slavery, colonialism, and the economic imperialism of global capitalism, I wonder if, like all human empires, its time has come. The Bible shows clearly that systems of world power rise and fall—or, to be more biblical, God raises them up and then brings them down, according to his own purposes in human history. No empire lasts forever. There are signs of the whole Western "empire" collapsing under the weight of its own idolatrous *hubris* and the mountains of debt which fuel our economies.[7]

But if and when Western power collapses, especially the USA itself, untold chaos, confusion, suffering, and loss will devastate not only the West, but the whole world. The global financial crisis of 2008 was a warning, but has anything been learned from it? Have those who precipitated it changed their ways? The COVID-19 pandemic can be seen as another warning—certainly giving us a vivid example of the fragility of human life. Since it was a humanly caused zoonotic event (a viral disease "jumping" from animals to humans), it will probably not be the last pandemic. If a virus can do such damage, what lies ahead through the relentless burning of forests and the destruction of species—of plants, animals, marine creatures, birds, and insects? Our polluted and poisoned earth, oceans, and atmosphere cannot sustain our merciless depredations indefinitely. Only God's faithfulness to his promise to Noah on behalf of all life on earth preserves us.

I am genuinely fearful for the future that my grandchildren face in the next half century of their lifetimes. I am not quite into Habakkuk's state of pounding, quivering, trembling physical collapse, since God spares us who are not prophets from "seeing" the future as Habakkuk did. And, of course, as I have emphasized throughout this book, I firmly believe in the living God who is sovereign in his governance of world history and will remain so no matter what lies ahead for my own small country, let alone for planet Earth and the human race. I trust in God! Nevertheless, this biblically anchored faith cannot take away the natural and justifiable fear of the ultimately disastrous consequences of human folly, greed, recklessness, and evil.

---

7. I have discussed this somewhat further in *"Here Are Your Gods": Faithful Discipleship in Idolatrous Times* (Downers Grove: IVP Academic, 2020).

Habakkuk experienced this too. Faith and fear go together. It's not so much that Habakkuk simply moves "*from* fear *to* faith" (in the words of the title of Martyn Lloyd-Jones's exposition). Rather, he moves from fear wrestling in *protest* to fear wrapped in *trust*. Fear is not eliminated by faith. Instead, fear is controlled, dethroned, and robbed of its paralyzing toxins by faith in the living God, whose most frequent command in the whole Bible is "Fear not." That's why Habakkuk can both give vent to his fear and in the same breath counteract it with powerful resolutions.

So, what could Habakkuk do?

He will do what God told him to do, way back in 2:3: "*Wait . . .*" Specifically, Habakkuk will wait for God to do what only God can do: restore the moral balance of history by bringing judgment on the wicked. This means that God will not only judge Judah at the hands of the Babylonians, but God will ultimately judge the Babylonians also for their excessive violence and cruelty. Now, in fact, it would take approximately another fifty years between the fall of Jerusalem to Nebuchadnezzar in 587 BC and the fall of Babylon to Cyrus in 539 BC. Thus, Habakkuk probably didn't live to see the day Babylon fell. But he waited for it—knowing that God would ultimately put things right in the outworking of his sovereign justice on earth.

"*I will wait patiently,*" says Habakkuk as he endures the horrors of invasion and siege and total national collapse, knowing that what he so much dreads will come to pass under the sovereign permission of God.

And so, Habakkuk moves from being the troubled, desperate, and impatient questioner when we first met him to the patiently waiting (but still fear-filled) believer in God's sovereign justice whom we now hear. God had allowed Habakkuk to take the first place (a position we may often find ourselves in), and God had responded to his pleas and questions and complaints. But God now calls Habakkuk to respond and be in the second place, and by the end of his book Habakkuk has got the message.

Resolved to Rejoice—in the Face of Terrifying Loss (3:17–18)

Waiting is one thing. Rejoicing is another. But the circumstances in which Habakkuk resolves to rejoice are appalling:

> ¹⁷*Though the fig tree does not bud*
> *and there are no grapes on the vines,*
> *though the olive crop fails*
> *and the fields produce no food,*
> *though there are no sheep in the pen*
> *and no cattle in the stalls,*
> ¹⁸*yet I will rejoice in the* LORD,
> *I will be joyful in God my Savior. (3:17–18)*

Verse 17 is quite well known (we even have songs based on it!). But those of us who live in the industrialized West find it harder to imagine the full horror of this description. Most of our food comes from supermarket shelves or delivery vans. All the complex story of agriculture, harvesting or slaughter, processing, preserving, and distributing is hidden from our eyes and is (usually) of no concern. The worst we face is needing to stock up over Christmas, or when there's a cold snap and the food lorries can't get through, or when a pandemic forces us into lockdown and we worry about the elderly and infirm, or when a shortage of truck drivers leads to empty supermarket shelves (or a lack of the multiple choices we usually enjoy). But we have freezers, we have canned goods, we have online deliveries, and we have kind neighbors . . . . It will be a long time before we in the West face the real starvation that still stalks some corners of the earth.

So we may not feel the full force of what Habakkuk anticipates here in 3:17. This is indeed a picture of the complete and absolute loss of all the sources of life and survival. Habakkuk is facing facts—terrifying facts that would very likely happen if Babylon invades his tiny country. This is what his list would mean:

No fruit or vegetables
No wine to drink
No olives to eat, or oil for lighting and cooking
No crops of wheat and barley, so no flour to bake bread
No sheep or cattle, so no milk or meat
No staple food of any kind
Nothing to support life
Starvation and destitution

This could indeed be the fate of Habakkuk's people under invasion and occupation. Conquering armies inflicted exactly this type of punishment upon their wretched victims in the ancient world, especially rebel nations such as Judah, which had sworn allegiance to Babylon. Burn the crops, slaughter the animals, root up fruit trees and vineyards, and starve the population. Or, in today's world, destroy the infrastructure; bomb the dairies, the hospitals, and the schools; burn the villages; incinerate people with napalm; poison the farming land with land mines; defoliate orchards and forests with Agent Orange; and reduce whole populations to absolute destitution.

War is hell. It always was, and it still is.

This horrific fate hadn't happened yet for Habakkuk, but he could mentally anticipate it. But in the throes of his imagination, he comes out with this incredible resolve in verse 18:

> *Yet I will rejoice in the LORD,*
> *I will be joyful in God my Savior.*

Now, in the book of Psalms we often find psalmists declaring that they are rejoicing. But they usually explain why. They are rejoicing *for* something that God has done for them or for some sign of God's generosity and blessing. But that is not what's happening here. Habakkuk is not rejoicing *for* something. This is rejoicing in the midst of . . . NOTHING. There would be, literally, no-thing he could rejoice in . . . *except God himself,* as Habakkuk says.

Habakkuk's joy is in his relationship with God, for God's own self as Lord and Savior, not just for the good things God gives or promises. Even if there is no such "good thing," he will rejoice in God alone.

Habakkuk faces the facts, but rejoices in the relationship.

This is an enormous challenge. And I have to say that I don't know whether or how I could honestly say what Habakkuk says here. I can only do it in my faith imagination, and I will trust that God can make it real if I ever come to such a situation.

I occasionally do a "reality check" with myself. What if I lost everything that makes it possible for me to serve God in the ministry he has given me, especially of preaching, teaching, and writing? Suppose, for example, that I were to lose my ability to speak and could never again stand and preach God's word? Or suppose I had a stroke and could no longer think straightly and clearly enough to write books? Suppose I was paralyzed in some way that made speaking or writing impossible?

If any of those things were to happen, would I still know that I am loved by God and can rejoice in my relationship with him? Would I be content with the joy of knowing that my life in God does not depend on what I can *do* for him, but just for who I am to him and who he is to me? All I can do is pray that it would be so, and that I could truly affirm Habakkuk 3:18. I also pray that in God's mercy this situation never happens.

A devastating earthquake hit Haiti in 2010. In the midst of the appalling chaos, a Western journalist, expressing the atheistic scepticism that easily rises in Western minds in such times, asked a woman sitting in the rubble of her home, "Where is your God now?" Her answer apparently came immediately, accompanied by some surprise at the question itself: "Where he's always been—right here by my side."

A friend of mine from All Nations Christian College, now

working in Burundi, once told me a story about one of his missionary colleagues. In the aftermath of the Rwanda genocide in 2004, she saw an old man with an empty bowl praying in a refugee camp—he had walked five days to get there. She asked the man what his story was. He was in rags and owned nothing in the world. Now in his 80s, he had seen his wife and kids hacked to death and his house burned down. Indeed, he was nothing and had nothing. But at the end of this horrific story, the old man turned to the missionary and said: "Madame missionaire, I never realized that Jesus was all I needed, until Jesus was all I had."

When I tell this story aloud, I find that I can't even speak these final words without a choke in my throat. This situation is beyond my imagination. Yet Habakkuk, facing such a possibility in his own imagination, determines to find God himself to be all that he needs and to rejoice in him.

Can you? Can I?

Resolved to Be Strong—in the Face of All Obstacles (3:19)

We now come to Habakkuk's final affirmation, his last great effort of will and intention. It's a great way to end a song ("*on stringed instruments*"), let alone a whole prophetic book!

> *The Sovereign LORD is my strength;*
> *he makes my feet like the feet of a deer,*
> *he enables me to tread on the heights.*

> *For the director of music. On my stringed instruments.*
> (3:19)

Once again, we notice how Habakkuk has turned his questionings and protestations into very personal faith in God. God is "*my* **Savior**" (v. 18; my emphasis) and "*my* **strength**" (v. 19; my emphasis).

Habakkuk has said that he is going to "wait," but he's not just going to *sit back* and wait! He is not retreating from the turmoil of the world, withdrawing from all its anguish and danger. This is not *passive* waiting. No—the waiting and the rejoicing of verses 16–18 are here channelled into energetic and decisive action. Habakkuk *runs* into action.

Look at those feet: Habakkuk is on the move for God!

The coming calamity of God's judgment on the wicked is no excuse for being paralyzed. Not at all. Habakkuk is a prophet (1:1). He's on a mission from God. So he will claim God's strength and keep striding onwards.

Habakkuk is probably remembering Psalm 18 again, just as he did in the central section of his song:

> [32]It is God who arms me with strength
>   and keeps my way secure.
> [33]He makes my feet like the feet of a deer;
>   he causes me to stand on the heights. (Ps 18:32–33)

Here is a big difference, however. Psalm 18 apparently portrays David praising God after some great deliverance and celebrating a victory over his enemies. But here Habakkuk is using the same words in the face of devastating defeat and destruction. He has nothing whatsoever to celebrate. Yet even in anticipation of this grim fate, *God's mission goes on*. Habakkuk will be faithful to the task God has given him for as long as God gives him strength to do so.

This, too, is a lesson for us.

In a world that seems to be falling apart in all directions, it is easy to fall into depressive apathy. Anything we think we can do for God just seems to make no difference at all in the grand scheme of things. I am easily tempted to ask myself, "Why do I go on preaching, giving talks and seminars, writing books, giving money to the church and mission organizations, and praying for those who serve God on the front lines . . . ? Why should I go on doing all those things day after day, year after year, and indeed for all my life if things just keep on getting worse and the bad guys keep on winning and the poor keep on suffering?"

When such feelings arise, it seems easier to revert back to the *opening* verses of Habakkuk than to take hold of this *closing* verse. The challenge of Habakkuk's whole book is to urge us to not get stuck in the rut of protest and complaint at the start (even though such words are valid and heard by God). Rather, we need to join Habakkuk on the journey that eventually reaches the faith, joy, and determination of his final words, even in the midst of his understandable fear in a collapsing world.

Another friend of mine from Colombia, who is among the leaders of the Langham Preaching movements throughout Latin America, was speaking about the horrendous social, political, and economic conditions in his country during a time of sharing and prayer with our team. He felt that he was enduring a "Habakkuk season." As he put it, *"Living by faith, without the blessing."* He and his colleagues were doggedly carrying on with their mission in a broken and collapsing context of great evil and suffering.

There is a real spiritual battle here too. The term "the heights" in verse 19 is an expression in the Old Testament that usually refers to "the high places," those elevated locations (whether natural or artificial) where the pagan worship of Baal took place, accompanied by all the depraved practices of that idolatry. The existence of these grossly immoral places was part of the very reason that God's judgment was coming on Israel.

So, perhaps what Habakkuk means here is that he will go on preaching against idolatry—the mission and task of all the prophets. With God's strength, he will *"tread on"* these high places. He will proclaim the supremacy and victory of *"the Sovereign Lord"* God of Israel over all false gods, whether the ensnaring gods of Canaan or the threatening gods of Babylon. His mission as a prophet was to tread underfoot the idolatry that was incurring

God's anger. So Habakkuk would keep running to do this. On with his mission—no quitting!

This, indeed, is what the mission of God's people still includes. In word and deed, our mission is to declare and demonstrate the redemptive sovereignty of the living God over all idolatrous systems, ideologies, and powers that oppose him and hold human beings in slavery. Say among the nations that the Lord reigns (Ps 96:10)! Heaven rules (Dan 4:26)!

In New Testament terms, this is the gospel of the kingdom of God.

Jesus is Lord!

We are consequently called and commissioned to bear witness to this cosmic truth in all God's earth, in all God's strength, and for God's sole glory.

So, Habakkuk ends with this astonishing trio of affirmations:

- I will *wait*, because God will keep his promises of salvation and justice.
- I will *rejoice*, because God will always be there as my Savior.
- I will *press on in mission*, because God gives me strength.

Habakkuk's journey began with desperate questions. It ends with triumphant faith and determination.

If our journey has a similar starting point, may it also have the same destination.

QUESTIONS FOR REFLECTION OR DISCUSSION

1. What does it mean to pray with Habakkuk for God, in his wrath (which is real), to remember mercy? What would God's answer to such prayer look like?
2. Is our ignorance of the Bible as a whole story (embracing the Old and New Testaments), as well as our failure to celebrate

it as such, one of the reasons for the weakness and failure of the church today in the face of the evils of our world? What are the symptoms of this, and what can be done about it?

3. In what ways, if at all, do the last four verses of Habakkuk (3:16–19) reflect your experience, emotions, or commitments?

CONCLUSION

As we bid a thankful farewell to Habakkuk, it would be helpful to summarize some of the key lessons we have learned on this journey. In this world of increasing fear, of accelerating cycles of human violence and "natural" calamities, what kind of people are we called to be as those who know the living God and have put our faith in his Son Jesus Christ? As we scan over these chapters again, we may feel challenged in at least these five ways.

WE ARE CALLED TO LIVE AS PEOPLE WHO LOOK FOR GOD AT WORK IN THE WORLD

In answer to Habakkuk's opening question, God says, "I am working a work . . ." So, having asked the question, Habakkuk now knows and discerns that God is still active and sovereign in his world. It's still very scary, but it's in God's hands.

So, like Habakkuk, we need the courage of discernment—to know and trust that God remains sovereign in the world of history and nature. We need to listen to the news with this perspective in mind. "*Look at the nations and watch . . .*" (1:5). Watch out for God at work. Discern the mustard seeds of the kingdom of God. Join Joseph in recognizing, sometimes with the hindsight which then strengthens our confidence in the unknown future, that even things that are intrinsically evil (and were intended by their perpetrators to be so) can be the means by which the overruling sovereign God can bring about that which is good (Gen 50:20).

WE ARE CALLED TO LIVE AS PEOPLE WHO LIVE BY FAITH

We may not know how or when, but the Judge of all the earth will ultimately do what is right—either within history in his acts of judgment and redemption or ultimately in the great rectification of the final judgment. God will deal with all wrongs and put all things right before he makes all things new in the new creation.

Trust me, says God. Go on *living by faith*—faith in the sovereign justice of God as well as in the sovereign grace of God.

This is a real challenge to us in these times. But it is an essential part of what "righteousness" means. It means having a right relationship with God that is based upon God's grace and salvation and is then lived out in humble trust and faithfulness to our callings. We are saved by faith, and we must go on living by faith as a daily choice and life-orienting stance.

WE ARE CALLED TO LIVE AS PEOPLE WHOSE PRAYER INCLUDES LAMENT AND PROTEST

Habakkuk stands among the many in the Bible, including many in the book of Psalms, who cry out *to God* in lament and protest at the evil they see all around them. But do we? Or do we just complain and protest to one another?

We often pray in our church services for our political leaders, and so we should, for Paul commands it (1 Tim 2:1–3). They need God's wisdom and strength. They need the gospel too. So, yes, we can and should pray *for* our rulers to come to repentance and salvation and to do justice.

But do we ever pray *against* our leaders? For the Psalms certainly do this when those in authority perpetuate injustice, lies, suffering, and poverty. The psalmists appeal to God *against* wickedness in high places on behalf of those who suffer the consequences:

> Arise, LORD! Lift up your hand, O God.
>> Do not forget the helpless. . . .
> The victims commit themselves to you; . . .
> Break the arm of the wicked man;
>> call the evildoer to account for his wickedness.
>> (Ps 10:12, 14, 15)

The Psalms are full of prayers like this—but do we ever hear them in church? That is surely part of what it means to pray, "Your kingdom come, your will be done on earth as in heaven."

WE ARE CALLED TO LIVE AS PEOPLE WHO KNOW THE STORY OF GOD—THE WHOLE BIBLE

Habakkuk rehearses in vivid poetry some of the great episodes of the story of his own people Israel—those mighty saving acts of God in their past. Habakkuk knows the story he is in—the story that we now read in the Scriptures. As he reminds himself of this story through a powerful "worship song," as we might call it, his hope and faith are refreshed even in the midst of his anger and fears. And so it should be for us. We should draw hope from not only knowing the story so far (from the Bible), but also from knowing where the story leads and how it ends.

We cannot avoid the realities of the story we are caught up in, because our world is full of sin, folly, idolatry, injustice, and suffering. That is the world's story. And if we focus only on this, we could easily get stuck in Habakkuk's opening questions. We would never get beyond the world we see around us—this fallen broken world that breaks our hearts.

But this book (and indeed the whole Bible) calls us to live by *another* story—which is not *separate* from the world's story but absorbs, embraces, and transcends it. This is the story of the redeeming mission of God promised to Abraham, Israel, and the prophets, accomplished through the life, death, and resurrection of God's Son, Jesus, and to be completed when God brings all of human history and all things in heaven and earth into reconciled unity in Christ in the new creation. This is our story. Are we living in it? Are we allowing that whole-Bible story to strengthen our faith and generate our joy, even in the midst of a collapsing or threatening world around us? Or has the Bible become just a box of random promise verses, like daily vitamin supplements, rather than the sustaining grand narrative that gives meaning and purpose to our life in this world and the new creation?

WE ARE CALLED TO LIVE AS PEOPLE WHO ARE ON A MISSION FOR GOD

Habakkuk is not going to just sit back and wait for God to intervene—no, he will run into action to continue his ministry as a prophet, depending on God's strength. As we have just seen, "the heights" probably meant the places of idolatrous Baal worship and all the immoral activity that went with it. Prophets like Habakkuk constantly spoke up against that idolatry and all its abysmally destructive social consequences. Habakkuk's mission, like ours, was to expose and oppose all the idolatry that produces such injustice, violence, and suffering, and to call people to repentance. He now plans to get on with that mission, with energy and determination, in the strength of his Sovereign Lord.

What's our mission? What's yours?

We certainly live in an idolatrous, violent, and scary world. In that sense little has changed since the days of Habakkuk. But in that world we are still called to be people of discernment, people of faith, people of prayer, people grounded in Scripture, and people active in holistic missional engagement in word and deed.

May we respond with the obedience of faith, knowing with Habakkuk that the Sovereign Lord is our joy and our strength.

SCRIPTURE INDEX

SUBJECT INDEX

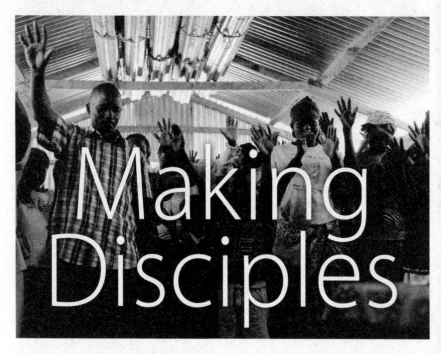